Focused on Spirit

A Journal about Spiritual Gifts

Serving Humanity

For my dear friend Theo, with lots of love and gratitude,
Laura

Laura O'Neale

Published by Your Light Within LLC

Copyright ©2013 by Laura O'Neale
U.S. Copyright Office – order #31051946
All rights reserved

Requests for permission to record, photocopy, perform or reproduce any part of this book should be sent to Laura@YourLightWithin.com

Cover Design by Laura O'Neale and Ion (John) Bogdan Dragutescu

ISBN 978-0-578-12065-2

Published in the United States of America by
Your Light Within LLC

Printed in the United States of America

First Edition

Will also be translated into Romanian and published in Romania.

With love and gratitude,
Focused On Spirit
Is dedicated to my dear parents,
Ion and Margareta

Acknowledgments

With love and gratitude, I give special thanks:
To the Divine Presence channeling through me and allowing me to connect directly
To Shaman Manin, for her teachings and guidance rooted in deep universal love, for passing on precious spiritual gifts from the Universe
To Shaman Diego, for his pure heart that allows spirit to work through him and help me and so many people make big steps in their spiritual evolution
To every person and every soul who is mentioned in this book
To Maribeth Decker, for being such a wonderful spiritual partner all along the way, and for her wonderful feedback that helped me finalize this book
To Hugh O'Neale, for valuable insights and especially, for being an amazing spiritual partner and true source of love
To Ion (John) Bogdan Dragutescu, for graphics and cover design
To Elisabeth Hallett, for line editing (author of *Stories of the Unborn Soul*)

Content

Content	7
Introduction	9
Part I: Spirituality and Oneness	15
My Guru in a Temple of Light and Dalai Lama's Teachings	17
Spiritual Love and Partnership	25
Love for Oneness	35
Part II: Going Directly to the Source	39
Transcendental Sparks of Light	43
Thank You Native Americans	53
Thank You Mother Africa	59
Thank You Lord Shiva	63
Thank You Shamans	69
Thank You Zamolxis	75
Thank You Lord Jesus	81
Part III: Manifestations of a life focused on spirit	89
Shamanic Birth	91
Self Healing Through Love	97
Spiritual Missions	105
Sacred Union	113
The Long Journey	117
Two worlds in harmony	131
How can we stay focused on spirit?	143
Part IV: Sacred Shamanic Ceremonies	163
Transcending Ego	169
The Tree of Life	187
Trinity	195
About the Author	203

Introduction

Beloved readers,

This book is for everyone who believes in the omnipresence of the Divine. Wherever you are on your spiritual journey, you might enjoy reading this book. It is filled with blessings, love, gratefulness, and bliss.

Ever since I was 19, I heard every single spiritual teacher that I met talking about the same thing: the importance of being focused. Some teachers explain what to focus on, others do not. In essence, they all know that the greatest duty we have while on Earth is to transcend the limitations of our egos, and the only way to do it is by focusing on spirit.

Through the years, I often wondered why focusing is so important. The more I started to open the doors of the unseen, the more I understood: the most powerful protection in this Universe is our heart's purity.

The more we focus on light, the lighter our heart becomes. When the heart is filled with light, only good things can come to us, and through us. We are divinely protected. We are more loving. We raise the vibration of our planet. We are better people, better healers, and better citizens of the Earth and of the Universe. We are at peace. We are happy. We are one.

Ultimately, the more we are accustomed to focus on light while alive, the more easily we will find the light when the time for our long journey comes.

Focused on Spirit is one of my journals, my personal 2012 shift, bringing into the world many of my spiritual realizations and worship in the last four or five years. Its content, however, is not presented in chronological order. For a long time, I just wrote down my spiritual experiences, dreams, and channeled inspiration.

My journal also includes ways in which people benefited from the use of many spiritual gifts. As a student of Multicultural Shamanism, I've been keeping such a journal to better understand how spirit works through me, and to learn precious lessons in the process. This is why the subtitle is *A Journal about Spiritual Gifts Serving Humanity*.

When I felt the calling to share my bliss, the structure of this book started to unfold, and the purpose of my sharing became very clear.

"Thousands of candles can be lit from a single candle, and the life of the candle will not be shortened. Happiness never decreases by being shared." – Buddha

Initially there were no poems in this book, not even where inspiration from spirit came with a rhyme. One day though, my friend HawaH, who is a yogi and a spoken word poet, encouraged me to write a poem to be published in a fabulous book he was compiling and editing at the time, entitled *The Poetry of Yoga*.

So I went home and wrote my first poem – the first one in this book, depicting, word by word, an amazing experience I had during a meditation session that followed a yoga session, several years before.

Writing that poem was a truly blissful experience, one that awakened my desire to transform into poems many more of my spiritual experiences, dreams, and insights. Poems seemed to be easier to read, and I found that they were giving a touch of beauty, ease, and grace to the existent stories I was ready to share in *Focused on Spirit*.

The purpose of this book is:
–To give many thanks, and to bring honor to the Divine
–To inspire you to seek your truth, to find your true knowing from a spiritual perspective of who you really are, of what this Universe is all about
–To inspire you to live a life of unity, respect for all creation, communion, and spiritual evolution
–To inspire you to find or follow your own spiritual bliss, and to participate fully in raising the vibration of the planet
–To inspire you to respect and to love everyone
–To reinforce the importance of spiritual tools we all have, and provide additional ones such as meditation techniques and empowering energetic expansion attunements that transformed my life
–To inspire you to see and live your life with its major events as a sacred ceremony
–To inspire you to nourish your pure heart

"I am blind and do not see the things of this world; but when the Light comes from Above, it enlightens my heart and I can see, for the Eye of my heart sees everything.

The heart is a sanctuary at the center of which there is a little space, wherein the Great Spirit dwells, and this is the Eye by which He sees all things and through which we see Him.
If the heart is not pure, the Great Spirit cannot be seen. The man who is pure contains the Universe in the pocket of his heart." – Black Elk, Oglala Lakota

As a Reiki practitioner, I am presenting the healing art modality called Reiki as a way to give, to bless, to offer light, and to connect with Spirit. You will see this in many of the messages presented in Parts II & III.

About the structure of the book:
Parts I & II bring inspiration and spiritual oneness. Here are deep internal realizations and messages that I have received with the help of the spiritual tools described in Part III (chapter: *How to stay focused on spirit?).*

Part III tells that any spiritual essence that doesn't manifest in the world is incomplete, is not fulfilled and fit for life on Earth. We do not seek spiritual essence just to be happy in our hearts, and continue to live an ordinary life. We seek a whole life, where the physical and spiritual existence reach harmony and conscious coexistence.

In Part IV there are the most profound experiences of my life, during sacred shamanic ceremonies. Universal truth is presented to me while experiencing life from a pure spiritual perspective. These experiences are presented just the way they were; however, no words could fully describe their depth. They are now available to you as a source of inspiration.

Many people might never encounter a direct connection or a profound exploration of spiritual practices that they didn't grow up with. In other words, a Christian might always be connected only with Christianity, a Buddhist might always be connected only with Buddhism, and a Hindu might always be connected only with Hinduism in this lifetime, and so on and so forth.

Focused on Spirit is not about religion, and it's not about promoting one belief system or another. This book is about being present, it's about respect, gratefulness, and acknowledgement of all manifestations of Spirit: the Divine we find at the core of any religion, and the Divine we find in our hearts.

About the cover: one day I sat in meditation, closed my eyes and asked what should the cover of *Focused on Spirit* depict. Soon, I saw the image of a child, and a light coming from behind. Her smile was innocent, joyful, and connected with Magic, just like children are. At the same time, she looked as wise as someone who still remembers the wisdom of ages from the other side.

In love, oneness, joy, and spiritual bliss, I invite you to read and breathe this book, and let it empower your spirit.

Be blessed,
Laura

Part 1

Spirituality and Oneness

My Guru in a Temple of Light and Dalai Lama's Teachings

When I was 19 years old, I met my first esoteric teacher, Alexandru. He taught me simple meditation techniques, and he let me discover their power and purpose. He was 91. Not long after we met, he joined the spirit world, but he continued to guide, protect, and teach me from the other side.

"Please heal me and teach me. Take me to the essence of my soul." – That has been my invocation to him at the beginning of my meditation sessions.

Through the years, there were times when I practiced his meditation techniques every day, and times when I did not. When I meditate every day, I can see a big difference in the quality of my thoughts, my dreams, my goals, my intuition, my ability to attract what I want into my life, and my ability to practice healing arts. What a transformative, transcendental experience! Thank you, Alexandru!

I noticed that the best time to meditate was after yoga classes. After concentration, stretching, and opening the chakras, the mind is already quieter, and the heart is more prepared to connect with the wonders of the Universe.

Looking at a wall of bricks that was "ugly" before
Right after my yoga class
Now I saw it all shiny like a crystal door
It was a mirror of my chakras

I went home knowing that I am now ready
To experience deep meditation
I lit a few candles – my temple is merry
Now I am sitting down in a lotus posture

My eyes are focused on one dot on the wall
This dot is the gateway to infinity and bliss
My breathing slows down more and more
My crown opens in a thousand petal lotus

Rivers of prana are flowing through my veins
My thoughts are leaving me one by one
Till there is no more worldly nonsense
Only peace and bliss… "It is done!"

"Be quiet, so I can create" – God tells me
Now I understand my responsibility
So I am not talking nor listening
I just am, and it feels like infinity

My aura expands more and more
I can see it in the "mirror" of the wall
And I feel my guru's spirit joining my energy
Because now it's in harmony

You and I unite in a strong bond
I'm holding a huge bowl of light in my hand
Healing light that I offer to all of us
Now *we* are all *one*, in bliss!

In a very deep meditation session, with my eyes closed, I saw Alexandru's spirit in a temple of light, in the air, above and in front of me.
He was sitting in a lotus posture, dressed in a white robe made of light, very radiant and powerful.

He showed me a purple light in his temple, to focus on. "Look here" – he said to me. He pulled the pain out of each of my eyes and from the left part of my brain. This pain was bothering me for a while from too much computer work.

I found myself breathing in energy from down the spine up through the top of my head, and then exhaling it in fireworks of stars through my crown chakra. From my root chakra to the Universe, it was a tunnel of light.

"Focus on my love" – my guru said. I felt so much oneness with him, with the spirit world, with the purple and white light. I came back slowly after a while, and slept like a newborn at night.

That was one of my most amazing connections with my guru's spirit, in deep meditation. After that, my life has changed – I became more focused on spirit.

My guru's meditation helped me follow my soul mission, and so I became a Reiki Master/Teacher. Then I met Rev. Bob Hickman, Shaman Manin and Shaman Diego, who have been teaching me more and more how to grow in spirit and how to serve humanity.

Years after seeing my guru in a temple of light during deep meditation, I went to see His Holiness, the Dalai Lama, presenting "Kalachakra for World Peace" in Washington, DC. I didn't know much about Buddhism and wanted to explore, connect, and find common spiritual roots.

I sat down in my chair, in an enormous room, with over 5,000 people.

HH Dalai Lama was on the stage, but too far away for me to see him, so I looked instead at the video recording on the wide screen, right up and in front of me. Immediately it reminded me of my guru in the temple of light.

"If you don't have a temple in your heart, you can't find your heart in any temple." – Dr. Wayne Dyer

The Dalai Lama offered a teaching on releasing materialism as a path to cease suffering. He was cleansing our energy fields, offered a prayer (chant) and then started the initiation.

As part of the initiation, he offered us sacred water. The water was passed along the rows for everyone to take a sip and put a drop on their head.

While we were all enjoying the sacred water, I heard thunder, and then the sound of a heavy summer rain. What a "coincidence"! Even more amazing was to go outside a half hour later and notice that only two or three streets around the building where we were all day were wet...

Dalai Lama taught us to meditate and visualize above and in front of us our own spiritual masters in the nature of light, crystal clear, very radiant. This clarity symbolizes the union of the magic body and the clear light.

I was amazed! That's exactly how I saw my guru, years before, during meditation!

The Dalai Lama explained that the whole purpose of meditation is to lessen the deluded afflictions of our mind and eventually eradicate them from their very roots. Again, I was amazed, knowing the benefits of meditation in my own life.

The next key point His Holiness made was to meditate on compassion, on loving kindness. "Practice altruism, the source of inner peace that leads to global peace. Be purposeful, and your mind becomes purified, enlightened."

Yes, I knew this is true deep in my heart! On my Reiki journey, as I started to practice distant healing as a form of meditation, I felt more and more peace and infused knowledge flowing through me.

I felt that healing brings love, love brings peace and peace brings oneness. You can read more about my Reiki journey in my book, *Reiki and the Path to Enlightenment*.

"Meditation on one point helps the mind release delusion and confusion, and mind chatter" – the Dalai Lama said.

Yes, indeed, the more I meditated, the more my mind cleared, my thoughts left me just like the clouds are passing, letting the sun shine.

Did my guru teach me Buddhism? I wondered. Alexandru taught me to meditate while fixing my eyes on one point. Alexandru told me that he had studied occultism in a secret German school, and Bhakti Yoga in India, but the essence of his teachings was the same as the Buddhist teachings.

"Expand kindness from the loved ones to everyone." – the Dalai Lama said.

Yes, the more I practiced healing arts, the more I loved myself and my closest ones, the more I found myself being able to love others, expanding and breathing the bliss of love.

> You and I will heal and grow
> Through our compassion and love
> For one another

Soon after I met Shaman Manin, she blessed me with the Quan-Yin-Cubed Attunement, a true gift from the Councils of Light. To let this beautiful energy run through me, I was taught to place a hand on my heart and say:

> I love myself
> I forgive myself
> I am at peace with myself
> Therefore
> I love you
> I forgive you
> I am at peace with you
> And
> I love the whole world

> I forgive everyone who hurt me in the past
> I am at peace with all that is

This mantra helped me so much through the years. It helped me step by step, to heal myself and help so many other people heal. In the beginning I had to fake it, especially the last part of it: "I love the whole world"; then, the more I kept being focused on spirit, the more I knew the truth of this mantra in my heart.

Jesus teaches forgiveness and acceptance. I grew up with my grandmother Roza reading His words, but I grasped them more later.

The basic precepts of Buddhism – do not kill, steal, indulge in sexual misconduct – are so much like the precepts of Christianity.

"Cultivate union, union in emptiness" – the Dalai Lama said.

My guru's meditation helped me find union in emptiness, which is true bliss. My mind, however, still has to learn more how to free itself fully.

There are deeper and deeper levels of emptiness and bliss that can be attained. Only in the last few years, the Peruvian Sacred Ceremonies led by Shaman Diego gave me an easier access to that emptiness and bliss.

Dalai Lama's teachings helped me feel the wholeness of all spiritual teachings I've been exposed to so far.

As a student of Multicultural Shamanism, I was so pleased to find how much respect I have for the Dalai Lama's teachings, and how much I feel the essence of Buddhism through his words. I am grateful and I give thanks.

> *"People take different roads seeking fulfillment and happiness. Just because they are not on your road doesn't mean they've gotten lost" – Dalai Lama*

Spiritual Love and Partnership

Spiritual love simply means loving people's divine spark of light, nurturing people's potential of becoming enlightened beings that are manifesting their soul missions in the world. It takes patience, acceptance, inspiration, support, and pure, unconditional love. It takes the knowing that at the soul level, we are all one. Loving others as we love ourselves is the recipe.

> *"Spiritual love is so great, it seems like there is nothing greater. And once you feel it it's difficult to feel anything less."-Wanakhavi, Reiki Master*

The good news is that the desire for such spiritual love is in everyone; it is just not awakened, or not shared. We can keep looking for that in people and water the seeds of true love in their hearts.

Spiritual love as a way of living life, is something that so many people have no faith or hope for; this is how life becomes empty, this is how people become unhappy, sick, and do so many things that take them even further away.

We are co-creators with God. Our lives transform through the union of spiritual family, which is allowing each and every member of it to grow and fulfill their life purpose, and accomplish a higher common purpose.

Who is our spiritual family?

We might never find details about our past lives, about the infinite journey of our soul, but when we feel pure joy in our hearts as we meet people, we can consider them part of the same soul-family, or spiritual family.

Some of them might be new soul-family members, some might be many thousand years old relationships. We love each other, teach each other, and support each other in different ways to grow and accomplish our soul-mission.

The essence of spiritual partnership is pure love. Souls who met perhaps thousands of years ago, are coming back together, through time and space, attracted miraculously like magnets, to teach each other more, support each other more in their spiritual journey, and accomplish a divine purpose they received, they chose, or will create together.

Have you ever been concerned about losing contact with someone by the changing of name, address, phone or e-mail? Well, when we have a soul agreement, we will meet even if we have been born in opposite corners of the world. Not to worry, spiritual love is like a Global Positioning System (GPS) – it will take you to the right place.

My first esoteric teacher, Alexandru, came through in a mediumship session with my spiritual consultant, Bob Hickman, and said:
"She is my little one!" – he began. "You have learned well, my daughter; I was with you as you wrote this book* and I will continue to be with you. If I had many students, there are few that understood deeply, as you did.

You have captured, in essence, all my teachings. You have written in a way that will allow many generations to come, and to see, and to know, and to hear the very experience that I thought to teach you, and now they will learn from you.
Your writing is giving me life on the Earth again.
It is your heart where I want your teachings to begin and to stay.
The books will come, yes, and they will be more, but my words, if they don't stay in your heart, have no value to anyone.
As long as you are true to your heart, my dear one, you will always have my blessings and I will continue to communicate with you.
You have heard my voice many times."

* The book Alexandru referred to is my first published book, *The Journey of the Colorful Stars*.

This message tells not only about spiritual partnership beyond life and death, but also about *pure love as being the essence, the catalyst of spiritual teachings, learning and partnership.*

"Love is the KI (Life Force) of the Universe" – Shaman Manin

If we indeed live thousands and thousands of lives, we had a chance to meet an incredible number of souls; each of them had the same chance, so the number of connections grows exponentially with each life lived. The web of love spreads and expands more and more, wrapping up the Earth in a web of light.

Directly or indirectly we all know each other; as souls, we are interdependent, interconnected, related with each other in one way or another.

Our parents, children, life-partners, lovers, friends, partners, and co-workers, are all possible spiritual partners. We create and magnify our spiritual partnerships as we follow our soul mission.

When we add to our loving relationships the awareness about our spiritual journey, and tools to expand our connection with the Universal Consciousness, our spiritual partnerships blossom even more.

***

Here are some examples of spiritual partnership, covering just a part of my incredible relationships or amazing connections between people in my life:

I had never considered my grandmother Mama Nana a spiritual partner till right before her death. Even though she had faith in God, and she was a loving and caring grandmother, I thought that through the years she didn't have as great an impact on my spiritual journey, as the other grandmother, Roza, had.

However, as I followed my soul mission and became a Reiki Master, I had the opportunity to serve and support her in getting ready for her long journey, and in the process, we became spiritual partners.

Our conversations about the journey of the soul, about the light she was going to see when she passes away, about the soul of my grandfather who was about to take her, would not have been possible without my training and without my spiritual consultant's teachings.

She actually gave me the opportunity to have my first magical experience of being in service during my astral traveling. Being sent by Spirit to give her a Reiki Attunement while asleep was a miracle sustained by our love for each other.

She also gave my mom – her daughter-in-law – the opportunity to become a master of care and compassion, by needing total care for almost four years. In one of my readings with Bob, he told me that my mom chose to learn about compassion in this life, as part of her spiritual journey.

Sharing this with my mom, she found more ease in her care-giving, and later declared her devoted care as being one of the most important sources of gratefulness in life. So, my mom and her mother-in-law were also spiritual partners.

"When you realize how perfect everything is, you will tilt your head back and laugh at the sky." – Buddha

*

When I first came to the United States, my parents and good friends from Romania were often worried – "You are there among strangers." In the beginning I only had a few family members/friends here, but actually I didn't feel surrounded by strangers, I felt surrounded by wonderful potential friends.

Making friends from all over the world was the first step; then, as I followed my spiritual pathway more and more intensely, many of my friends did so too, and many more new spiritual friendships were born.

When you communicate from soul to soul, all cultural, political, religious, racial barriers vanish.
When you step aside from what you've been conditioned to believe about yourself and others, you realize that there are an infinite number of similarities and just a very small number of differences.

We are Universal beings, and we need mirrors to see that. I have seen myself in so many mirrors – my friends from all parts of the world! Now I feel and I know that I lived everywhere through them.

Therefore home is everywhere on Earth. The boundaries disappear, the ancestors are expanding, and the religious beliefs are blending. Unity becomes reality. I am grateful to God for all the "mirrors" in my life.

The whole planet Earth is my home, because people from all over the world have a home in my heart.

*

When my dear Greek friend, Niko, who was like a father to me, unexpectedly passed away, I was praying for his soul, and his voice came deep in my heart telling me: "Make them laugh" (he was very funny, he was the source of joy for everyone around);
"Take care of Ana" (his wife) – another message came through.

For his funeral, I was called to buy two bouquets of white roses. I didn't know why, till the end of the service, in church, when he came into my mind saying "One for me, one for Ana." So I gave one to his wife, from him!

Next day before going to bed, I wanted to pray for Niko but I was tired and almost fell asleep; all of a sudden I heard deep in my heart Niko calling me. So I got up, prayed, lit a candle, drew the Reiki symbols and sent him empowering attunements.

Then, I quieted my mind, waiting for a sign from Niko. All of a sudden, my right hand became heavy; then, I saw Greek characters....
"Gosh, Niko, why would you want to write through me in Greek, when you know English? I don't know Greek!"
Then, it occurred to me that he wants my writing – my book – to be given to his community, as a proof of his eternal life.

Then, I saw my grandmother Roza taking Niko's hand in hers. Guidance and protection on the other side were the energetic meanings of her gesture.
I love you, Niko! Thank you for being a light in the world! I honor our new spiritual partnership.

My experience is that the more I followed my soul mission, the more soul-family members I met, or recognized between my existent loving relationships. All it takes is to be focused on spirit, to pay attention to the calling of the soul.

***

As one becomes committed to his/her spiritual journey, more love and support are required constantly, as sources of sustainability. As our wings are growing, we need the power of community.

> *"You are here to enable the divine purpose of the universe to unfold. That is how important you are!"* – Eckhart Tolle: spiritual teacher and writer

The process of spiritual development is much faster as we share our experiences and support each other. *It is vital to share, in order to make thoughts become things.* Sonia Choquette teaches this concept as a tool of developing intuition. Unless we put into the world the subtle, gentle intuitive messages, they can be lost in between so many other thoughts.

When we grow spiritually, and especially during the process of intense transformation associated with self-healing, awakening, experiencing the divine powers working through us, we need to have someone to share with, someone to listen to us, someone to understand, accept, love us, offer us support.

Sharing is almost a must, but it is not wise to share in a negative environment. I don't recommend to anyone to share their new spiritual experience with negative people. Thoughts of distrust, envy, anger, fear, and so on would be coming out of them and bombarding the new butterfly, bending its wings.

The power of a spiritual community sustains safe and constructive sharing.

Spiritual partnerships are the beginning of something greater. God has a bigger plan for all of us, which will be revealed in divine time.

Little by little we are becoming part of a global network of light workers, and truly make a difference in the world. It is no coincidence that people with harmonious vibration meet and become close to each other.

Where there is love, there is no need for barriers: we can trust the power of love talking and acting through us. When people are concerned with managing boundaries, they disconnect from their higher self, they are not themselves, and therefore they don't really know what to do, and feel uncomfortable and insecure. Spiritual partners simply choose to live a wonderful life, from inside out.

If you feel isolated in your spiritual journey, if you're afraid to open your heart and talk with anyone about your dreams, your spiritual gifts, your gut feelings, your visions, know that you're not alone, that out there are so many others just like you, and seek out networking. It is so important!

Resources are more and more convenient. If you don't know anyone, at least start with internet networking, such as Facebook.com or meetup.com. Choose freely whom you want to spend your time with. Also, you might be meant to be a teacher and to create your new soul family. Ask for divine help and your soul family will come into your life, one by one.

One day Ananda, who had been thinking deeply about things for a while, turned to the Buddha and exclaimed: "Lord, I've been thinking – spiritual friendship is at least half of the spiritual life!"

The Buddha replied: "Say not so, Ananda, say not so. Spiritual friendship is the whole of the spiritual life!"

Love for Oneness

Oneness is a function of the crown chakra – being one with all creation. Oneness is the ultimate goal of humanity.

We still have a long way to go, yet it is achievable; we all have the choice of following our higher self, and attaining the highest levels of self-love, love, acceptance and peace, from the inside out.

As we heal ourselves from anger, fear, low self-esteem, and guilt, we can love ourselves more and more; as a result, we can love "others" more and more, till, one day, there is just *us*.

> *Where there is love, there is peace.*
> *Where there is peace, there is Oneness.*
> *Where there is Oneness, there is God.*

As we all know, there aren't even two people on this planet with identical fingertips. Why did God create us to be unique? Being so, we can call ourselves different. Is "being different" the same as being better? Not at all; in God's eyes, we are all perfect.

Our higher self also knows that we are perfect. Only the ego has the need of comparing and proving itself. We are a little different on purpose, so that together we can bring a broader experience back to the Creator.

"Beyond any reasonable doubt, we each share the ancient name of God in our bodies in the most intimate way imaginable. Each fiber of muscle, each crystal of bone, the tears that we shed – all are God." - Gregg Braden: Spiritual philosopher of ancient and indigenous traditions.

Jesus Christ is my Master Guide, and I am calling on Him for myself and anyone who accepts His healing. If I am to be in any kind of altered state of consciousness, or between life and death, I know that my faith in Jesus is so deep; I can still call on Him. In other words, if I should lose my mind, He is still there, in my heart.

Perhaps no one would give up such deep faith, regardless the name of their Master. However, we don't have to be exclusive, but rather do our best to open up and experience the power of oneness.

Along the way, I've passed Reiki initiations to people from many different religious backgrounds. During these initiations/attunements, I prayed and asked the Higher Power to give a Reiki attunement to my students and as an offering of Light, to their Guardian Angels or their Master Guides – just like I did for my own Spiritual Guides and Master Guide.

As a result, not only are my students benefited by automatically connecting Reiki with their faith, but my connection with their Spiritual Guides and Masters is strengthened as well.

Now I feel respect, love, and a personal connection with all Ascending Masters, with Lord Shiva, with Native American Guides, Jewish Guides, Caribbean Guides, Egyptian Guides, grandfathers and grandmothers of many different cultures.

Oneness in diversity expanded through my love for diverse people into love for all their diverse spiritual guidance, and became oneness in spiritual essence. Acceptance of differences, unconditional love, the acknowledgement of that essence in each and every person, in each and every Spiritual Master Gide, brings a blissful communion at the deepest level. I am grateful and happy from the inside out.

The power of wholeness in my heart is too overwhelming to be kept a secret. Therefore I have published this spiritual journal of mine to encourage you to fully open your heart and love every_one_.

Awareness, confidence, acceptance, humbleness, love, faith, and oneness are gradually attained in each of our hearts, and I believe that their depth is infinite, as we follow our infinite spiritual journey.

> *Love for oneness is the greatest way to be Focused on Spirit*

Part II

Going Directly to the Source

What our mind knows is what we were taught. What our soul knows is what we receive directly from source.

With a little bit of practice, and with a pure intent, we can all access the source. It is a beautiful experience of gratitude, oneness, purity, truth, and pure love.

When I am focused on spirit, inspiration flows. How do I know it is coming from a source of light? The answer is simple: by the way I feel.

The voice of spirit comes through a state of bliss.

In this chapter are many raw messages I received through transcendental states of consciousness
– During sleep followed by invocations and prayers
– During individual or group meditation sessions
– While meditating in my copper pyramid
– During drumming sessions
– While praying
– During shamanic journeying
– While relaxing in nature
– While listening to icaros (songs for healing recorded by a shaman) or to relaxation music

The messages in quotes are presenting the voice of spirit I heard in my heart.

Your Vision will become clear only when you can look into your Own Heart. Who Looks Outside, Dreams; Who Looks Inside, Awakes – Carl Jung

Meditation stays at the core of all spiritual development; when we add to it the purpose of healing, its power grows tremendously.

Spiritual gifts such as clairvoyance or clairaudience often awaken and develop more and more without focusing on the desire to have them, but by serving humanity through energy work and by passing initiations/Attunements.

A good and powerful intent attracts good and powerful guidance. My intent is:

Love, Joy and Peace for every<u>one</u>

In my little copper pyramid, typing up insights after meditation

Transcendental Sparks of Light

"You hold the pen between your fingers
The same way you keep your hand
To make the cross and say Amen
Or to do Reiki on yourself
Write words of light!
You are responsible for what you write
You give power to the thought"

*

I am a blossomed tree
I am at peace because I have roots
And I can focus on my flowers now
My flowers are my gifts to you
You're far away, I cannot see you
But you can see my flowers
In the photos, books or dreams
And that's giving me even more peace.

*

Meditating on Klaus Schulze's music
I am *Floating* between the stars
I am the eagle flying above the mountains
I am the panther running through the fields
I am the fish swimming in the ocean of light
I am the fire dancing in the dark
I am the wave, the ocean, the land
I am the wind blowing through your hair
I am transcending, I am here!

*

While planting tomatoes with a friend
With my hands filled with dirt
I found my childhood's peace and joy
Of being connected with Mother Earth

*

In my dream I was peacefully flying, not too high
I was using a chair and a remote control
A few people saw me and
Asked me what I was doing

I told them that I am testing a device
And they started to chase me
Wanting to steal it from me
So I started to fly faster, to escape

Soon I realized that the chair was heavy
Pulling me down toward the ground
And the remote control occupied my hands
Preventing me from swimming faster through the air

My enemies were getting closer and closer
So I remembered to have courage
And apply my own inner knowledge
So I threw away the chair and the remote control

I was lighter
And found myself flying higher and higher
Turning left and right
Just with the power of thought

The chair and the remote control
Were just an illusion
And a limitation
Of my own ability to fly

They were keeping me away
From exercising my faith
But now I know how to fly
Very high

*

"Everyone is responsible to hold the space for miracles."

*

Holding river stones in our hands
During group meditation with spiritual friends
After a while I felt my stone was heavy
But when I put my hands in a prayer posture
I didn't feel the weight of the stone anymore
Even though it was between my hands
And I understood that any
Heaviness in life disappears when I pray

*

"Breathe three times to learn in spirit
Each of these important truths:
Respect, Love, Forgiveness, Gratefulness
They are all Divine gifts
Without God you won't feel this."

*

"When you can't find peace
You just need to breathe."
When I breathe deeply I can swear
Love is in the air

*

"Thank you all for your courage to be born."

*

I put essential oils on my body
And lay down in the sun, on the grass
I felt the oils activating on my skin
And a vortex of energy opened
I realized that essential oils are a portal
Of energy from the Universe
They attract the stars of light
Just the way the plant does

*

"If you don't know your parents
Love them anyway!
They are just metaphors for your
Mother Earth and Father Sky
Before your mother and father, I was!"

*

"Love and respect my son"
A mother said to me
"My son is your son
Our son! One! One!
Your son, my son
It doesn't matter, they are one!"

*

I was a drop of water
Tumbling down the street
Toward the ocean
Filled with sparks of light

The metaphor is
The return to the *one*
The trip toward the spirit
"I am one with the ocean of love"

*

Here I was at Sovata, Romania, in a lake with a high concentration of salt, sulfur and calcium. The water kept everyone at the surface. I found peace and at some point prayed and ask that an Angel will come and pour Light in the lake, for everyone who enters to heal.

One of my friends was watching, not knowing what happened, and took a photo... the Light is here, and in no other photo taken before or after that moment.
Thank you, Angel!

*

In the past I thought that
I am not humble enough
To think that the Universe
Absolutely needs me

But the truth is that
The Universe needs everyone
All I needed to learn at that time was
That I am a cell of the tree of life

As part of it
We are all one
We are all needed
And very much loved

*

"What's written now
Will remain through eternity
Just be love and let me be"
God said to me

*

"The roots must be strong and healed
For the flowers to blossom
Love yourself more."

I have solid roots
I see colors if I grow
Wild toward the sky
I grow because
I know the stars

We are sister stars
There are plants like me
On other planets

*

Oneness means that we all have
The seeds to be anything
From the lowest to the highest
Human being that ever walked on Earth
What we manifest depends
On what seeds we water
What we choose
And how much love and faith we have

*

"The letter L is a shape that
Defines the path of the light
Down through your crown and
Out through your mouth

Blow the light you receive
To do healing and to love
This path of light is the connection
Between God and Earth

Blow stars of light from your guts
You just have to breathe
And give the stars of healing
That's your path."

I gave the stars of light to our teachers
For them to help us all
"Remember to blow stars of light

From your guts to each soul"

I gave the stars to my father
And he looked younger
My mom, with love I kiss your hand
Mother and father, you are so loved!

*

"Transcendental meditation is
Wisdom out of prison"

*

In my vision, I gave blessings
To my God-daughter
She is four years old
And she loves the stars of light
Then, I gave her advice
But in spirit she stopped me
And told me
"Have respect!
We, the kids, know it all
We lived here before."

*

In my dream I was in a room
Filled with many people
A purple orb appeared
Everyone was looking

I lay on my back
And started to sing
A song that I was never taught
But my voice was different

I wish I had such a voice
It was vibrating with pure love
At a very high frequency
And I was levitating

Not too high from the ground
The purple orb started to fly
Parallel with my body
And then entered my forehead

*

"You are here for all
To understand oneness and peace"

Thank You Native Americans

My spiritual consultant, Bob, told me that my two Native American guides, Silverbell and Black Crow, will send me on missions to liberate lost souls. A few months later, while visiting my relatives and friends in the Baltimore area, I woke up one morning with a joyful feeling for my Native Guides. Nothing distinct, I hardly noticed the feeling....

My cousin Dan invited me for a walk and meditation session in a beautiful forest, ten minutes away from his house. I was under the weather, but it felt like a great way to start the day, so we went.

At some point we had to cross a creek in order to continue our journey. Two girls riding horses were coming from the other side. One horse was brown and the other one was white. Seeing it, I knew in my heart that my spiritual teacher was announcing something great that is going to happen, but didn't really express it in words.

The white horse stopped in the middle of the stream and was hitting the rocks on the bottom with his leg. It felt like he was communicating something to me.

After they left, my cousin and I continued our journey till we arrived in a beautiful spot, with a wide opening and a wooden bridge over the creek. I sat down on the bridge, looking at the beauty of nature around us, taking in the peace and harmony of the forest. My cousin sat down maybe thirty feet away from me.

As soon as I rested enough, I started to do my daily invocation:
"I am so delighted to receive all the blessings the Universe has to give me!
"I am welcoming God in my life, and all His Councils of Light – healers, teachers, guardian Angels, Jesus Christ, my Native American guides…"

It took me a few minutes to go through the entire sequence of invocations and energetic expansion attunements. When I finished, I offered them to my cousin too. He loved the energies very much.

Then, I closed my eyes again and saw a spiral of colors – as if I entered through a gate into a different dimension. My Native Guides came to mind. They had their hands lifted up, and both had spirals of light running through their bodies.

"You must enjoy being here; I'm so glad – Enjoy!"
Aaaaaaa-Oooooo-Aaaaaa-Ooooo they started to chant, and so did I, aloud, in the same time with them.

Almost instantly, another twenty to thirty Native American spirits appeared, as human shapes of light. A few words in a native language I didn't understand crossed through my ears. I was fascinated. Wow, was the forest their place before?

Then, a little girl came to me. She wasn't made of light, she looked real. "She was lost, and she's still lost. Give her a Reiki Attunement," my Higher Self said.
"All of you, please connect to this little girl, so you'll all receive this Reiki Attunement," I told the crowd.

All insights were tuned into the spirit of my Native American guides. The feeling of Oneness was powerful, loving, and blissful.

So I gave a Reiki Attunement to the little Native American girl, and as soon as it was completed, she disappeared in the crowd, now looking just like the others – made of light.

Then, a huge Light-Being appeared through the branches of the trees – the Spirit of the Forest. It was more of a knowing – the knowing of my guides.
I opened my eyes for a moment, hoping to see the same thing, but everything disappeared.

As soon as I closed them again, a Native American young man with long hair and warrior outfit came toward me, riding a horse. He was made of light too. Getting off the horse's back, he stopped right in front of me, and I knew from all my being that he was my love, in a past life.

The completion was profound – pure peace. We just came to see each other again for a second, and offer each other a gift that would honor each other's spirit.

"Be blessed! Be blessed! Be blessed!" I said, while surrounding him in pure white light. He opened his hands and a little white dove flew toward me. Bliss!
Completion! Love! Peace!
Everything disappeared.

Opening my eyes, I looked at my cousin, who said:
"Laura, I just saw a guy with long hair riding a horse that was coming toward you."
Wow, we both had the same vision at the same time!

After a few quiet minutes of peace in bliss, out of the blue, I asked my cousin: "Would you like to receive a Reiki Attunement?" and he said, "Yes, I was about to ask you for that." So he received it, and his spiritual guides received it too.
We were grateful for the spiritual abundance and high vibration of that place.

"Are you ready to go back?" he asked me as we finished.
"Wait, there is one more thing," I said.

Closing my eyes again, I saw four Native Americans around me, cleansing my aura, doing healing on me. I needed that and really felt great afterwards. I fact, I had been fighting a cold for the past four days, which totally disappeared in an instant.

Then, I saw a few elders, sitting in a circle, smoking pipe; and for the first time in a vision, I saw Sitting Bull, the Native American from Shaman Manin's painting, who I knew is part of our soul-family.

Sitting Bull

He was speaking in his native language. Power, harmony, and wisdom were his energetic imprints. I was so honored!

"What gift would you like me to give you?" I asked.
"We are here. Just keep loving us," he said.

So deep, so simple! Of course I'll always love them! Deep in my heart, there is no other way! *We are one.*

My vision was complete. My cousin and I left, and on our way back, we found the white horse's shoe!
"This is good luck!" my cousin said, filled with joy.
"This journey opened new possibilities."
Indeed, when our spirit creates, new possibilities appear.

Thank You Mother Africa

The drum's beat is making our hearts sing. The bliss is flowing. "Africa! Give thanks to our mother Africa. She is our mother." I feel it through my veins.

The stars of healing are coming down on a spiral of light, through my crown, and out through my mouth.

I am blowing the blessings over these amazing drummers in the Malcolm X park, in Washington, DC, in honor for our roots, in honor for the blissful feeling of being in a cradle of love, transcending through time and space. Thank you stars of light, for blessing Africa's children!

*

Alemayehu, my dear spiritual friend
I am younger than you
And I am from Romania
But in a past life I was your mother

You were drinking my milk
Now you are an enlightened
Spiritual mentor who protects us
And makes our hearts sing

But you asked me for a
Reiki initiation
And I gave it to you
With love and admiration

Drink my milk, master and God father
It is Knowledge and Knowing
It is transfer of fluid light
It's so simple, and pure, and bright

Yes, indeed, I was your mother
I love and respect and know you
I was very young
When you were born

We grew up together in spirit
And with my eyes closed
While listening to the drums
I saw my old wrinkled black hands

In an ancient cave
Somewhere in Ethiopia
We lived very long
Singing the same song

Our roots of light
Grew through the Earth
And met again
On a different land

Our home is now in America
But our mother was, long ago, Africa
Thank you, mother
For bringing US back together.

Thank You Lord Shiva

Right before giving a Reiki II attunement to a Hindu friend, I asked God, Jesus and my Reiki Guides to give an attunement to her and to her favorite God, Lord Shiva. The attunement for Lord Shiva had the purpose of offering Divine Light. As soon as the attunement took place, I felt a bolt of energy all over my body.

In that state, I thought again about a group meditation that I had been trying to put together for a while. It felt like Lord Shiva was guiding me to give it the final shape.

It was Divine... The name "Magic Oneness Meditation" came to me. At the end I made a beautiful heart of Light that grew so much, it encompassed the Earth.

This event helped me realize for the first time that passing Reiki attunements to people from all religious backgrounds gives me the opportunity to connect with their Spiritual Masters. It is a true blessing.

Below is The Magic Oneness Meditation.

I am with a group of people, some more familiar with meditation, some trying for the first time. After cleansing the room, lighting candles and inviting personal guides in, everyone in the meditation circle stands up for a few minutes. We imagine that roots are growing down our feet, deep into the ground, and all negative energy goes down, to be transformed by the Earth in new, purified water.

Then, while breathing in, we visualize a spiral of Light cleansing all our energy centers: above crown, crown, third eye, thought, heart, solar plexus, sacral, root, legs and feet. It's like a tornado of light moving clockwise. We are breathing the light through the crown chakra. As we are breathing out, we visualize any negative energies or useless thoughts getting out of us, counterclockwise.

We repeat this exercise three times, or even more, till we feel calm and free of thoughts. This is a powerful energetic expansion attunement channeled from the Councils of Light by my teacher, Shaman Manin. It is called the "Cleansing Healing Thought Form Attunement."

Next: each person asks for Light, connects with Divine Light, and visualizes golden white light flooding their bodies. Once we do so, any communication that follows between us will be primarily through Divine Light. Reiki practitioners can also draw the Reiki symbols on their palms and ask for Reiki Energy.

Next: we are sitting comfortably in a circle, holding hands. We do a basic chakra meditation: from root to crown, we visualize each color, each of our energy centers, and we take one deep breath for each transition: red, orange, yellow, green, blue, purple and white.

Once we get to visualizing the heart chakra, we visualize the green lights blending and forming one big heart chakra. We stay there and we feel our sacred union.

It's been said that at the end of humanity's life on Earth, this is how we'll all leave the planet – as one, big heart chakra. The essence and ultimate purpose of Jesus's teaching – Unconditional Love, will help us leave our planet as a big heart chakra.

To continue our Magic Oneness Meditation, we focus on our throat chakras, and we visualize blue electrical currents of light between our throats. We enhance our level of communication, as well as our connection with our spirit guides.

Then, when we get to the third eye, we visualize indigo currents of light between our third eyes. If only two people are participating they can look straight in the other person's third eye as long as they can keep their eyes open without blinking. This is quite an experience for both souls!

Then, once we get to the crown, first we see our own white light. Then, we imagine that we're all surrounded by columns of huge Diamonds, and Light and energy circulate between the columns creating a portal of propulsion out there in the Universe (this is also one of Shaman Manin's Attunements – the Diamond Attunement).

We visualize white light from each of our crowns growing up, blending, then splitting up only to go in all directions and form the Heart of Light, which is going to come back together at the base of the heart of light, below our bodies. At the same time, each one of us continuously receives Light through our crown chakras.

We dissolve into Light and we are created again through Light. We feel the bliss!

Then, we declare our intent even further – to encompass the city in a heart of Light. The diamonds are working. We are the Heart of Light, together.

Then, we declare our intent further – to encompass the continent in a heart of light… then, the whole planet Earth. The diamonds are working, spinning energy.

How far do we want to go? We can continue…. And meet stellar beings and give them all our offer of Divine Love and Light.
We are one with the Universe. Love! Peace!

We slowly come back. We declare our intent to fully come back. We may not want to…but we have to come back…. We open our eyes slowly. We clap our hands together using just the tips of our fingers, three times. It will help us come back to "here and now."

We give thanks to Lord Shiva and to our Spiritual Guides.

Breathe and Trust! Your Light Within is the key to your deepest, peaceful place, where all the answers are!

Thank You Shamans

In this chapter are a few poems depicting deep, meaningful spiritual experiences encountered during shamanic journeys guided by Shamans Diego, Sara and Manin.

These amazing Shamans come from three different cultures; however, they lead us to the essence of our souls in very similar ways.

Shaman Diego was not present while my group of spiritual friends and I went on the first shamanic journey shared below, however, his healing songs helped us shift into a higher state of consciousness. That evening I had also passed eight Reiki attunements, and that sent me into a higher state of consciousness. The icaros, our collective energy and shared spiritual love, helped us all to have amazing insights.

>   Meditating with my Reiki Master friends
>   We were listening to the Shaman's songs
>   I went back to my childhood village
>   And walked the path toward the fields
>
>   Once there, I transformed into a seed
>   The soil was soft and it felt good
>   So I immersed deep in the ground
>   Waiting for the rain, to sprout
>
>   It was moist and warm after the rain
>   I sprouted, and it was so much pain
>   I started to grow but didn't know

What kind of plant I am

My roots were growing
Transcending Mother Earth
And I came out in South America
In the middle of the forest

A healing plant surrounded my belly
And shook me till it healed me
Then the spirit of this magic plant
Touched my mother, and pain was taken out

As my mother and I were healed
I felt profound peace
And holding my mother's little hand
I took her on a journey through the Universe

She looked with wonder and she felt
That everything is perfect
She saw the infinity of life
And now she's confident

We came back into our bodies safe
And now I clearly hear
My grandmother Roza's words in my ear
"I love your mother, I am here"

*

Sara, beautiful Shaman, led us on a journey
We went down, deep into the ground
Through the thick roots and the hard rocks
Into the belly of the Earth

We cleansed in the river of fluid Light

Then, rose through an underground ocean
And arrived on a peaceful and quiet path
Paved with beautiful stones and sand

The guardian of the place was there
Thank you, Sara, for creating the space
For me to reconnect with my Native Guide
He was drawn by your Native songs

The guardian was an old but strong shaman
With long white hair and light leather wear
I embraced his presence and then dared
To ask that he take me to the three chambers

In the first chamber, I found a green tarot card
And felt that I have the green mother Earth in my heart
"Right now I am in the middle of it, and I'm safe"
I found my peace and gave many thanks

In the second chamber there were many gifts
It was paved with crystals of all colors and shapes
And there were other sacred objects
But I took a bracelet made of black shungite

In the third chamber were three animal guides
A big eagle, flying with me above my life
A dolphin, surrendering with me to the ocean of Light
And my dear dog, teaching me unconditional love

Having to pick just one, I picked my dog
And came back up through the Earth
I gave thanks to the guardian – my dear Native Shaman
And returned in my body, filled with love

Now I will replenish myself

By meditating every day
While in the shower of light
Connected with the Shaman in my heart

I will focus on being nurtured and connected
And loving unconditionally
This practice will keep me peaceful
And the bracelet will keep me grounded

It was so beautiful! Thank you, Sara, you are so powerful!

*

"Sirius is the other planet"
Shaman Manin told me, telepathically
"When your pineal gland is lit
It communicates with Sirius
And that's where we met"

Thank you, my dear Shamama
For reminding me of our other home
Our love is so old
We know each other for so long…

*

Shaman Manin invoked the Councils of Light
And asked for our guidance and protection
And then she led us on a trip through the Universe
For us to discover new layers of perfection

We were flying higher and higher
Piercing through the rainbow of the seven colors
We passed through a black hole

And found ourselves on a huge golden ball

I offered my love and respect to the Councils
They pulled layers from my forearms
To my elbows I was filled with negativity
From hands-on healing on my clients

The Councils blessed me and gave me a star
To hold in my hands and bring into my heart
A crystal and a rose were given to me
To help me go further on my journey

I came back toward the Earth
And carried all these great thoughts
Down to the core of our planet
And back through my feet, like a magnet

Thank you, dear Shaman Manin
For taking us with you on this journey
To the stars and to the Councils of Light
Now I feel the Universe in my heart!

*

"Seeking God inward or outward
Is just an illusion
Oneness is the answer
Of any Divine vision"

You and I have
The same light inside
We are but a reflection
Of the stars

Thank You Zamolxis

In 2008 I visited the Ialomicioara's cavern – one of the most beautiful in Romania. I was sitting on a rock, praying, meditating, and giving thanks to the spirits of our ancestors, the Daco-Getae. They were known to be there, since the cavern was actually a powerful energy vortex.

I remember what a wonderful energy I felt, and how magical the visit in the cavern was.
As my friends and I were getting ready to leave, a tourist who pretended to have psychic abilities approached me and told me that while I was on the rock, Zamolxis's spirit came around.

I would not have known where the powerful and beautiful energy came from, however, a part of me was skeptical. At the same time though, the possibility made me feel honored and curious to connect more and know more about Zamolxis.

At the time all I knew about Zamolxis was that he had been considered to be the sole God of my ancestors, the Daco-Getae. He was known as a holistic medicine man, also skilled in the arts of incantation. He taught the belief in immortality, so that the Daco-Getae considered that they were going to Zamolxis after death.

Through my friends, who have a very strong respect for Zamolxis, I found that many organizations and individuals were doing research, and many things are now believed about Zamolxis.

Some were saying that he used to live in a cavern, and at some point he wasn't seen by anyone for about three years. Others were saying that Jesus Christ might have met Zamolxis, who gave Him his blessings and shared his wisdom.

I would have loved to know that it was true, and it wasn't impossible, after all, since Zamolxis was alive during Jesus's time. However, it is hard to believe anything like that without having any insights in the matter.

So I prayed that one day I will have a vision that will bring me more clarity about Zamolxis, the God of my own ancestors.

I returned to the United States, and a few years went by after my visit at Ialomicioara's cavern. Caught up in my daily life, I forgot about Zamolxis.

It was a wonderful Thursday evening, and a few of my spiritual friends gathered for weekly group meditation.

I was very tuned into my spiritual self that night, at peace and very relaxed. We started our group meditation session with OM-ing and invocations, and then continued with quiet meditation, holding hands.

About fifteen minutes later, with my eyes closed, I saw an old man, with long white hair and beard, making fire. He was in a cavern, and in the fire's shadow on the wall of the cave, he was getting messages from God.

"Who are you?" I asked.
The answer came deep into my heart: "I am Zamolxis."
I was surprised, amazed, and honored at the same time.
"Where are you now?" I asked.
The answer came internally, clear and powerful:

> *"Don't look for me outside*
> *I've been always in your heart*
> *I am the flame of God*
> *The light inside the cage*
> *And it takes much courage*
>
> *It takes the knowing*
> *That we are all responsible*
> *To always focus*
> *On our light inside"*

Minutes of silence followed, and somehow I felt that I was in the cavern myself, making fire. Zamolxis allowed me to transcend, and feel, and know his truth.

> I have learned that it's not so hard
> Not seeing the stars at night
> Nor the sunlight all around
> When I see the love of God
> Shining from the inside out
>
> I have learned how huge
> Were the responsibilities
> Of my people's God, Zamolxis
> Holding the space for all of us
> To be the light, from inside out
> And to know our essence
> Transcending the darkness

Zamolxis allowed me to see and feel and know his essence. Moreover, thousands of years after he joined the spirit world, he told me that he is in me.

More than ever, I understood and knew my roots, and I felt connected in a more meaningful and profound way with all Zamolxis's sons and daughters – the Romanian people.

Zamolxis was the God of our ancestors, and whether or not we know it, we are carrying his essence in our hearts, through eternity.

Meditation time was up. With three OMs, we returned to here and now. One of my dear spiritual friends, a medium, told me that she saw a lot of fire energy with me during the entire session.

Amazing! I thought, giving her thanks.

That night I had a vivid dream, with Jesus Christ making a miracle. He was with the blind beggar, and He was teaching the crowd:

> *"The blind man lost his sight*
> *To lose his ego, and look inside*
> *Now the blind will see the Light"*

Thank You Lord Jesus

In my dream I was on a huge platform
And all people were there
On the right was the furious ocean
On the left was a train going nowhere

Everyone was scared, trying to escape
But there was no one there to help
And there was no way to fly
Through the tornado in the sky

I went toward the old, still train
And there was a woman looking sane
She told me "they" have something
To help us evade

We went underground
And there was another train
A supersonic, extraordinary vehicle
For all of us to be saved

But as we were looking at it
The train vanished in front of our eyes
And the woman said, disappointed
"I'm sorry; we actually can't help you guys"

We realized it's really a serious danger
And I left, going downstairs, deeper
In a storage room, filled with old stuff
Where a wooden holy cross was on the ground

A mouse came in and hit a pot
That was up on a shelf
The pot fell and cracked
Right on Jesus's head

Jesus woke up and got off the cross!
And then I didn't see Him
But felt His presence on my left
And my sense of peace was sublime

I asked Jesus to come with me
And save us all from devastation
He came and everyone was there
Waiting for the end of all creation

In my hands I had a lot of pictures
And browsing through them I found my mom's
"Jesus, can you save her?" I asked
"*She is saved*" Jesus said. It was done

Browsing again through the photos
I found one with my father
"Jesus, can you save him?" I asked
"*He is saved*" Jesus said. It was done

Browsing once more through the photos
I found one with my God-daughters
"Jesus, can you save them?" I asked
And Jesus showed me a photo in my hand

It was a photo of me flying high above
Carrying the two little girls in my arms
They were safe and so was I
"*They are already saved*" Jesus said.

What an extraordinary dream about the power of faith! The hidden room represents the subconscious mind. Jesus was there, forgotten on the floor, between many other "things." As he "awoke" in me, everything became possible. All I had to do was to ask Him for help, and it was instantly given to me.

My God-daughters were already saved… what did that mean? I wondered. Thinking about my childhood and theirs, I found the common thread: as a child, my grandmother Roza planted the seeds of faith in my heart.

In return, I've been planting the seeds of faith into the girls' hearts, even before they were born, through Reiki, prayers and continuous love and blessings.

Our faith is the engine, the light, the power, the omnipresent source of energy that doesn't let us fail. When I am focused on my faith, everything is possible.

Focus on your faith, dear ones. Focus on your blessings, on your bliss, on your love. The Universe is Abundant. Let's open the door of our hearts.

*The power of faith is the power of love.
It helps all of us fly above the storms of life.*

*

It was Easter time. My love for Jesus is beyond words. During the Holy Week I felt lots of sadness for his suffering. On Good Friday, I got a bouquet of white roses for my Lord.

Saturday, I created a sacred space, immersed into deep meditation, and prayed for Jesus.
In front of me were the white roses, a lit candle, and Jesus's image.

I imagined that I am in the cave – His grave, holding His feet between my hands. His body seemed to be dead, but it wasn't stiff.

Maria Magdalena was my inspiration – she had put essential oils on his body. In my mind, I thought that if I were she, I would have asked to stay with Jesus's body for three days. I would have taken the risk; if no one returned to open the door and let me out, I would have died in peace.

Through the millennia, people have chosen to risk their lives for things that were less important. My heart was filled with love; I just wanted to be there with Him.

My love for Jesus opened my energy channels, and my hands became hot, as they do when I offer healing sessions.
It was so humbling to be a tool in God's hands for loving Jesus… "Isn't my vibration too low to serve?" – I felt so small, but my love and compassion were appreciated – I felt welcomed there.

"Just be there" I heard my own Higher Self.

"Are you dead?" I asked.
Jesus was not dead, He had a near death experience – I knew.

He was initiated and knew how to maintain life, but chose to die for us and fulfill His mission... he almost succeeded, and now His body needed a miracle to come back.

"I am here" I heard a loud answer coming from within Jesus. It was loud in me too.
Soon after, I saw light coming down through the ceiling over him. Then, huge entities of Light were placing their hands on Him. A Light was also coming in around the stone at the entrance.

Now Jesus's spirit was in the cave, watching His own body, and watching me holding His feet between my hands. All of a sudden, I heard His Heart beating, from within Him and myself, just like I heard His voice before.

My palms were burning; all my chakras were wide open. I was in a different dimension; I was truly not trying to heal Him, but just loving Him, fully allowing the energy to flow through me.

My sweetheart came and joined me; one of my hands was on his crown and one on his heart chakra; one of his hands was on my sacral chakra; we created a circuit of healing, we gave each other what we most needed; our hands were really hot; he felt the energy flow, holding the space for me – he is an amazing spiritual partner.

My eyes were closed, and the vision continued. At some point, Jesus came back into His body. He got up. The Light removed the stone so he could leave the grave. He was shiny, made of Light, in his long robe, with his head covered.

Telepathically, I asked: "Jesus, may I have a family?" knowing that now He will leave to a place where I can't follow him. "Yes." Then, I asked Him to help my sweetheart in his efforts. Jesus blessed us. Then, He stepped out of the grave, and His last words to me, telepathically, were:

"Just tell them that they are all Jesus"

The vision stopped. The energy flow stopped too, and I came back to here and now; my sweetheart felt that our hands were getting cold. We were dizzy with overwhelming energy and bliss for a while.

In my reflection about this incredible vision, "they are all Jesus" was not a religious advertisement to become Christians; it's the confirmation of our imminent evolution, till we will all reach His level of vibration, His power of Love.
When and how? We don't need to know…. But just to live a life of love, and faith.

*

I was in California, in a hotel room
My sleep was so deep
And in my dream, a voice I heard
"Jesus died in California"

I started to search for Jesus
Walking on an unpaved path
Till Jesus rose from the dust
With three Lemurian crystals in his hand

One was green, the other two were clear
All were sparkling with divine light
Green is the color of the heart
Holding the power of healing and love

Jesus plugged the crystals into my heart
And I didn't feel any pain
Instead a huge wave of love and light
Started to flow through my veins

In my dream I started to say
"I am Jesus's daughter"
Three times, till I woke up
Ever since I feel even more loved

This dream was so vivid, it felt like I was back in time, back into my own memories.
I thought about it for a long time, and one day I heard that Lemuria is thought to have existed in the Pacific, by California's coast.

Jesus Christ might have had several incarnations, as I read in a book later on. If that is true, it could be that in one of them, He lived and died in Lemuria... we might never know that for sure, but the way I felt when Jesus plugged the Lemurian crystals into my heart completely changed my life.

Thank you Lord Jesus!

Part III

Manifestations of a Life Focused on Spirit

Shamanic Birth

One summer I went to Trinidad with my sweetheart. It was the black leather turtle's season for laying eggs. We went to the beach and witnessed the miracle. We learned that while laying eggs, the turtle was in trance. We were able to pet her, without her knowing it. I got closer and did Reiki on her. I looked in her eyes and saw the infinity of the ocean. She wasn't there; she was into the oneness of the deep waters. She was listening to her instincts, letting them do their work.

We have so much to learn from these creatures. We, the humans, lost so much of our instincts by exercising mainly our left side of the brain, which is rational, analytical, performing, judgmental, but full of fear and on its own.

> *Relax, to learn how to be a mother*
> *Give blessings to all the mothers to welcome your children*

Every woman has a birth shaman within. When the time comes, that shaman awakens. If you are a woman who's contemplating future birth-giving moments, do not fear. Instead, learn how to surrender, and let your birth shaman take over and guide you through the labor and birth process.

> *"I" cannot be a mother. Only <u>we</u> can be a mother*

This is a message I received from spirit. "Who are *we*?" you might ask. The answer is: you and your shaman within.
This shaman is one with the wisdom of ages. She has the experience of all births around the globe; she is connected with the Universal Consciousness of birth as Sacred Ceremony.

How to access the Shaman within? You might ask.
The answer is: surrender to your intuitive self. You have to allow the right side of your brain to work, and max out your intuition, your ability to have a trance-like experience. Do not think, do not fight, do not rationalize, do not count, and do not fear. Give up control and allow the miracles of oneness to unfold. Just breathe rhythmically and peacefully, and focus on spirit.

*

The time has come. The future mother dreams her baby's laughter. She wakes up still hearing the happy and crystalline voice.

I stayed inside of you and grew and now I will be born in light

Later that day, after nine months of daily meditation and conversations with her yet-to-be baby, the contractions begin.

Message for parents-to-be:

*"Meditate at the unity candle
Lift hands together and
Make light in your hands*

And ask your child to come."

What a wonderful way to start hours of labor to follow. All this time, professional medical care is not required. This is the time for the mother to be in her sacred space, just with her partner and/or doula.

The contractions are occurring more and more often. The mother is prepared: she trusts her body; she trusts her guides and her caregivers. She is filled with joy, and she uses the pain to strengthen her affirmations:

I am focused, peaceful, safe, and divinely protected.
I am surrounded by love.
My child is gentle and wise, and is coming out naturally, with ease.
I am one with my Birth Shaman within. We are giving birth to our child with ease and in the best conditions for my body and the child.

Through breathing, she transforms each painful contraction into a powerful reinforcement of successful birth-giving. When it hurts, she keeps her spine straight, she takes a deep breath, she looks straight ahead at a single point, and then, as she is breathing out she says: "Welcome to the world my dear baby; we love you!"

The light is dim in her large room. There is a circle of lit candles all around. She is listening to drums – rhythmic beats that help her stay in a light trance, and also give more power to her root chakra.

Her partner is with her. They dance slowly at times. They look in each other's eyes. If she loses her rhythm, her partner helps her come back into it. Her partner is breathing rhythmically, looking in her eyes; she follows. Her partner is calm, so she follows.
She is connected to her subconscious mind; therefore she is very easily open to gentle suggestions. Her partner may say at times in a very gentle tone: *"You are strong; you are peaceful; you are connected with the infinite wisdom of your shaman within."*

A cascade of ecstatic hormones* unfolds through the mother and the baby. All of a sudden, the mother enters a much deeper level of trance. She might throw up, her eyes might roll, and she might look lost. She is not lost, she has merged into the infinity of spirit, and she is having a divine experience that should be fully experienced in a sacred manner. She turns inward. Do not disturb her by telling her what to do. She is listening to the Birth Shaman within.

Now it's time for the baby to come out. The mother is allowed to give birth with privacy, patience, and the intimacy of those she feels most comfortable with.

She sits up, squatting, and concentrates on her breathing; straight spine; focused eyes, while practicing a tranquil and peaceful breath.

Breathe to give birth
Children are stars of light coming through
The mother's crown-root tunnel of light
Focus on spirit
Focus on light

Welcome into the world, dear little one. You are now in a human body, experiencing life on Earth. You now have a straight spine; you have eyes to see and ears to hear. Use them well. Live well.
Love yourself, love your parents and dear ones, and also remember your Mother Earth and Father God. You are a child of the Universe, given into your parents' care. Be blessed!

The mother holds her child on her chest, skin on skin. She is singing a song of love, and tears of joy are falling down her face. They are surrounded by family and many beautiful angels. A new chapter of life starts. Be blessed!

In the face of possible psychological challenges following delivery, here are a few messages from spirit to focus on:

Message for the new mothers:
You gave birth; you must forgive
Remember how blessed you are
Every time you get upset
You must relax and meditate
And create reality for you and all

Message for the new fathers:
Fathers are responsible to hold the light

*Note: The following hormones are working in tandem during natural birth:
- Beta-endorphins – help the mother to fall into the birth trance and to feel less pain during labor
- DMT, known as the "God-seeing hormone," is released at birth creating expansive spiritual consciousness in both the baby and the mother. The only times this hormone is being released by the pineal gland are: birth, birth-giving, death,

near-death experiences, as well as during Sacred Plant Ceremonies. The release of this hormone alone makes natural birth a Sacred Ceremony.
- Nor-adrenaline – creates the initial bonding upon emergence
- Oxytocin – the love hormone, causing the child and the mother to fall deeply in love with one another
- Prolactin – the mothering hormone, released during labor and breastfeeding; it facilitates breastfeeding, nurturing, and love

Medicated birth interferes with the release of these hormones.

*

I am deeply grateful for the opportunity I was given to volunteer as Reiki practitioner and doula in a hospital where integrative medicine is embraced. Helping mothers, partners, and family members to stay focused and confident during labor has been of great value for everyone.

The flow of Reiki through the mother and the baby still in her belly has the most joyful, pure vibration. Baby moves, mothers find peace and a deeper connection with their little ones. I am always asking them to put their hands on their bellies, and I'm placing my hands over theirs. "Talk to your baby. Give good energy to your baby. Welcome your baby with love."

Thank you God!
Thank you mothers and fathers!
Thank you, little ones!

Self Healing Through Love

As most of us have heard before, diseases are just an effect of a cause that most likely comes not from the physical realm, but from our emotions, interpretations, response to stress, worry, resentment, anger, guilt, and other negative feelings and thoughts. Sometimes the cause of a disease is more deeply rooted in our karma.

According to the chakra system, each of our seven major chakras is responsible for the good functionality of specific organs in our body. Imbalances in the chakras go hand in hand with negative thoughts, emotions, and furthermore, with physical illness. You can find a full description of all chakras and how to balance them in my book entitled *Reiki and the Path to Enlightenment*.

Below are a few examples of causes and effects I have seen in people in my life, Reiki clients, or myself through the years:
–Anger or long-term tense situations can lead to heart attack or stoke
–Resentment, lack of forgiveness of self or others can lead to cancer
–Excessive, constant fear and/or terror, can create colon problems
–A blockage in the ability to communicate, such as having to keep a terrible secret, can create throat problems, including cancer
–Constant stress and overwhelming mental work can lead to diabetes
–Hating someone can lead to heart issues

–Not wanting to hear parents fighting, or simply living in denial, can lead to ear problems
–Being judgmental can lead to autoimmune diseases
–Emotional turmoil, especially in a relationship, can lead to catching a cold
–"Inhaling" parents' emotional turmoil in early childhood can cause a child to develop asthma
–Worry can lead to respiratory issues
–Negative thinking/expectations about life can create fear of reproduction, therefore sterility
–Fear of losing financial resources can lead to heavy bleeding and hemorrhages (either by having "accidental" cuts or accidents, or through the monthly cycle for women)
–Lack of self-acceptance or identity issues can create sterility
–Unresolved karma inside the family can lead to congenital diseases in children
–Past lives ended by violent death can bring recurring unconscious memories, affecting the areas of the body that were affected and/or caused death in a past life.

These are just a few examples. For a more comprehensive list of possible causes of disease please read the book *You Can Heal Your Life* by Louise Hay – it can literally change and even save your life.

These unpleasant lists are not what I want to leave you with as you read this chapter.
To lack good health always involves, at some level, lacking love.

To be focused on spirit means to be focused on love – self-love and love for all creation.

Below are a few self help tips on how to heal the causes of disease. Reiki is also a wonderful tool, helping to heal on all four levels: physical, emotional, mental and spiritual. However, while not everyone yet has received the Reiki initiations, this simple recipe is always possible to follow.

HEAL THROUGH LOVE:

Heal your relationship with your parents and all other people in your life
Embrace the possibility of being in excellent health
Accept reality for what it is and for what it is not
Let go

Treat yourself well
Hear the voice of your heart, the messages you receive during sleep or during the day
Read self-empowering affirmations, such as "I love myself"
Observe your thoughts and don't indulge in negative thinking
Uplift your spirit; focus on beauty, love, and light
Give with love and compassion; create good karma
Have the courage to speak the truth

Love fully and unconditionally; you can only grow stronger
Oooooooommmmmmm daily, at least three times; it's not against any religion
View the world through the eyes of an innocent child
Evolve spiritually, purify your heart and mind

*

A very common reason for many diseases is to have unresolved issues from childhood, usually with parents or a close caregiver. It is amazing to see even older people, whose parents have long ago passed away, still running in a vicious circle of negative emotions ever since childhood or teen years. Unless we make a conscious effort to resolve such issues, no distance will be efficient enough.

Ask yourself where you are standing in this regard, and take time to heal your past.

In my own life experience, like most people, I was dealing with unresolved issues from childhood. They were all illusory, created by my own immature mind, by my own ego, through interpretations rooted in fear, not in love.

At some point I started to have bad dreams, such as ugly water in the basement of my house, getting into dirty waters, etc. These dreams were telling me that there was some disease in "the basement" of my body. The cause was also in "the basement" of my life, coming from the roots of my life.

Yes, dreams are very important, and if we pay attention, we can get valuable messages. These messages never come too late. They come mostly when disease hasn't even manifested yet in the physical realm enough to be identified by traditional medicine.

Meditation is an amazing self-awareness tool as well as the dreams. If everyone would meditate and would bring awareness into their bodies, diseases would never be discovered too late.

This is a very good reason for me to invite you to meditate daily, and from time to time, in your meditation, to bring your awareness inside your flesh and bones, into your blood and organs, into each cell of your body, and hear the messages you are given.

Very gently, the information was there for me – at a deeper level I knew that I had a health issue.

With that in mind, I went on a retreat in the mountains and spent time meditating and reflecting on my life, my childhood, my early life experiences, my interpretations and perceptions of reality as a child and teenager. In that quiet, peaceful place, surrounded by lit candles, in my vision, I was told by spirit:

> "After respect comes love
> You must respect your origins
> Respect your roots
> Respect yourself
> After respect comes love."

Respect? I thought about it for a while, and realized that indeed, perhaps in my foolish, childish mind, I had not really respected, accepted, and fully loved my origins, my roots, my wonderful parents, just the way they were and just the way they were not.

Instead, I had wished many times that I had been born to be a man, not a woman, that I grew up in different circumstances, in a different time and place in the world, with democracy instead of communism, with open borders instead of closed political doors and minds, with more women's rights, with parents of a different health condition or a different mentality, with tolerance and embracing for spirituality and multi-nationality… are you familiar with this attitude of loving more everything that is different than what you were given?

With tears in my eyes, I realized that my lack of respect, gratitude, and appreciation was all an illusion, and that everything was perfect just the way it was – with good and bad – because it helped me grow stronger, it helped me remember my soul mission, it helped me want to seek spiritual enlightenment, and it helped me learn patience and acceptance, and unconditional love. What bigger and better blessing could I ever want?

Filled with gratitude, I repeated aloud three times, while breathing in deeply, bringing the words down from my mind into my heart:

> I respect my country!
> I respect my roots!
> I respect my mother!
> I respect my father!
> I respect myself!

> Mother, forgive me! I love you! Thank you!
> Father, forgive me! I love you! Thank you!

Right away, I heard the voice of spirit again, this time helping me understand the roots of my past self-destructive tendencies, leading to bad life choices, which finally led to serious health issues:

> "After respect and love for parents comes respect and love of self."

Aha! So that was actually the very root of all my suffering, imbalances in the astral and the physical: not enough self-respect and self-love... Finally I really got it, and now it was natural for me to say:

> I love you mother
> I love you father
> I love you daughter

Like a movie, many bad choices I had made in my life had been finally understood, forgiven, and moved into my life chapter called "learned lessons." All of them had the same roots: insufficient self-respect and self-love.

Once the mystery was resolved, misery dissolved.

Soon after that day, my health started to improve, the quality of my life improved, my whole life experience shifted for the better.

I still needed to use Integrative Medicine (both energy work and western medicine) to fully heal at the physical level. Also I needed to give up eating junk foods, full of toxins that were poisoning my body little by little for so many years. In that healing process, which took a while, I knew there was no reason to worry, for the roots of my disease were already removed.

I felt free to take a deep breath. I started to truly live in love. This liberation was sublime.

A few years later, I was amazed when I found something about the ancient Ho'oponopono tradition: they were cleansing themselves with these four phrases:

"I love you. I'm sorry. Please forgive me. Thank you."

*

Please take your liberation seriously. If nothing else, you will live a healthier and happier life. Isn't that enough motivation?

Furthermore, to be focused on spirit, we must have pure hearts and clean minds. To be of service as healers, we must take the responsibility to first heal ourselves.

Release, detach, eject and shield! – Shaman Manin

Spiritual work and complementary medicine should not be a substitute for traditional medicine. There is nothing better in many cases than traditional medicine when it comes to treating the effect – the disease manifested in the body; but to really heal ourselves fully, we need to heal the cause.

That holistic healing, involving body, mind, and spirit, will transcend this body's existence and will reflect in future incarnations. Everything that is truly healed does not have to be experienced again. Everything that lingers could follow us through lifetimes.

It's simple, pure, and beautiful: we can heal through love

Spiritual Missions

My teacher, Shaman Manin, receives homework from the Councils of Light* all the time. Sometimes she gets lost on routes and soon she sees a car accident where she sends Healing Energies. Any time something happens, and apparently it doesn't make sense, it ends up that she was actually sent to be of service for guidance, healing, or soul release. She is on a mission every day, and also every night, during her astral traveling.

Councils is a broad name given to those beings from the Inter-Galactic Federation of Light, the Healing Councils, as well as the Ascended Masters, Prophets, deities, and beings from many dimensions, galaxies, and planets that are channeling energy through Shaman Manin for the Highest Good of Humankind.

The more we talked, the more I was amazed and inspired by the ways in which spirit works through Shaman Manin for the highest good of all. I wanted to be on a mission too, and live a purpose-driven life, guided by the Councils of Light. Any of us can do it. All we need to do is to be willing, and to use a few simple tools. In the process, we are never alone.

These tools, also called energetic expansion attunements, are available to you too, in the form of vibrationally enhanced images and invocations. You can find some of them on www.veinsofsilver.org as well as in Shaman Manin's books.

They can't bring any harm and are not against any religious belief. The invocations can be customized to fit anyone's faith.
They are blessings you might want in your life. The sequence offered to you in this book is a comprehensive set empowering all energy centers, all chakras, and each cell of our bodies, and can be found in the chapter entitled *"How can we stay Focused on Spirit?"*

As soon as Shaman Manin shared these invocations with me, I started to use them every day, and my life changed for the better within weeks. I was full of energy, optimism, confidence and joy, happy with my health, my inspiration, my teaching and healing practice.

After about six months of practicing the energetic expansion attunements daily, and practicing lots of Reiki work – both healing and teaching, I started to receive homework from Councils too. In this chapter you will find examples, and the lessons I was taught in the process.

*

At the coffee shop, a woman was crying. I approached her and reminded her that she is a beloved child of God and she's never alone. While talking to her I was running the Energetic Expansion Attunements for her.

About twenty minutes later, she said that I must be an angel because she had felt like she wanted to die, and my intervention shifted her intention toward hope. With tears in her eyes, she smiled. I knew that the Angel she was talking about was working through me, and I smiled back.

I've learned to not be shy, and follow my impulse to offer help even to a stranger.

*

Once I missed the bus when I so much needed to get to my destination on time, and had to wait for about ten minutes till the next one came; I got in and sat down. At the next stop, a very old and sick man got in, on a wheel chair, accompanied by a caregiver. His face was covered, as he perhaps suffered from asthma, and I could only see his eyes – the eyes of a dormant soul who was tired and hopeless in his old body.

In an instant, it occurred to me that I didn't miss the first bus by chance. Taking the old man's hand between my hands, I prayed for him and ran all attunements, for the highest good of his soul. I didn't say a word, but looking in his eyes, I was the witness of a miracle happening with him: sparks of love, joy, hope, and connectivity with God were now coming out of him. He was awakened to a different reality other than being a hostage of his own body; he reconnected with spiritual joy. I had done nothing but open my heart and allow the Councils to work through me.

I've learned to love through silence.

*

I was on a business trip in New Mexico. The best thing that happened to me was meeting a wonderful Navajo family and spending most of my free time there with them. Three generations, all amazing and beautiful.

That morning I prayed to my Native American Spiritual Guides to help me meet a Native American family. They did, and my fulfilled wish came with homework.
First I met a young man, his wife, and their beautiful child. We started a conversation about natural healers, and all of a sudden he felt that his mother was meant to meet me. He had a bad dream about her health and wanted her to see a healer.

The mother came to my hotel room, and for the first time in her life, the elder Navajo woman accepted healing from someone who was not Navajo. That didn't happen in the beginning, but only after our group meditation together, when I quietly asked in my mind my Native American Guides to *love their daughter through me.* Minutes of silence followed.

Then, the Native woman told me that she had changed her mind, and accepted my offer of a Reiki Session. I was honored to assist her in removing negative energy that could have caused a serious disease in her body, and felt guided by my Native American Guides the entire time during the session.

I have learned to step back and be patient, while asking guidance from the guides of the one in need.

*

A friend of a friend asked me to go visit one of her friends whom I had never met and to give her a Reiki session; the person in need of healing had been stuck in her house for many months, unable to walk much; she had suffered an accident, hurting her head, and now was forced to be by herself in the house.

My list of priorities was overwhelming; however, I felt a strong calling to go, and even cancelled a massage session which would have been a good financial deal and walked for half an hour through a blizzard, to offer help to a stranger, for free.

The calling was strong – there was no place for a "no." I felt the guidance and teaching of the Councils flowing through me. While she was telling me what had happened, between her words, I read the cause. I wrote in a notebook affirmations that would help her shift her magnetic attraction of future events. I suggested that she think about certain events and interpretations of events in her life. Then, I gave her a Reiki Session. As the Reiki Energy was flowing through me, more intuitive guidance came through, about the causes of her condition.

A couple of months later, she showed up at my meditation group, vibrating with energy and happiness; she said that our session was the key unlocking all her "doors." Little by little, she recovered fully. Moreover, she felt that by going deep within, forgiving, healing, analyzing her life, meditating, practicing affirmations, she was now spiritually reborn to a new life – a spiritual one. In the following year she took all Reiki levels with me and became a Reiki Master, and one of my dearest friends.

The whole experience revealed a new possibility for me: to combine Life Coaching and healing arts (Massage, Reiki, and Shamanism).

New soul missions are being born as we open our heart and follow the Divine Guidance.

*

It was around noon, when everyone in my office heard the noise of a car accident. Looking out the window, we saw a motorcycle rider in the middle of the street, and people gathering around him. The shift occurred in me immediately. It felt like I was guided, almost like I was flying, and I got downstairs in no time.

With my hands above him, I prayed from all my heart: "Reiki Guides, Jesus, Healers, Masters, please help him!" He was unconscious but alive. The crowd was gazing as usual, and without even thinking, I said "Pray with me!" They did, in many languages, as they were a very diverse group of people, till the ambulance came.

The ambulance personnel asked us to clear the way. I kept sending Flood Light, Reiki and prayers to him, to the emergency attendants and the ambulance from across the street.
This is when I called very powerfully on Councils and said, "Councils, please send Flood Light."

I gave up the need of feeling, seeing, getting proof… and surrendered to the higher powers in a way I had never experienced before. Then I returned to the office and kept sending healing light for another half hour. I was very dizzy, as never while sending healing.

It was weird because it felt like the energy was waiting, but at some point I felt a lot of heat, as if it was flowing heavily and it crossed my mind that he woke up.

Then, I disconnected, feeling very tired. Later, walking home I kept saying: *"He will live, and he will believe!"* All I knew from the police was that a few hours later he was still at the hospital, which was good news to me. They said the hospital would not tell me anything so I didn't even try to call.

That day I got a new goal – to work with the emergency room or teach as many of them as possible about how to use Reiki and the Energetic Expansion Attunements.

After a while, I found that the hospital has a Reiki Volunteer Program, and signed up for it. Many wonderful stories of hope, love, and rejuvenation are perhaps being shared by the patients who received Reiki while in the hospital.

I will share just one hospital patient's feedback, which is a wonderful fact and metaphor at the same time. With tears in her eyes, the patient told me: "I have asthma and can't breathe. In the last 24 hours I was put on life support ten times. Your touch helped me take my first deep breath in the last three days."

When we allow a Higher Power to work through us for the Highest Good, miracles can happen. All we need is to have faith and to let love flow through our veins.

Sacred Union

Everything that belongs to our Earthly existence is meant to be temporary. Everything that is God-like is meant to be eternal.

We are spiritual beings in an Earthly body. We have been given a body and the opportunity and delight to enjoy our Earthly existence. Therefore it is wise to accept both the eternal and temporary parts of ourselves, and find balance between the two.

When it comes to relationships, to make them last we need to bring spirit – the eternal, into play. Otherwise our relationships tend to be temporary just like everything else that is of the Earthly existence.

So, the secret of a spiritual union is to focus on spirit together.
Whatever spiritual practice a couple might take on, it will help the two surround themselves in a protective, solid, and blissful veil of light.

Some might pray together, some meditate together, some do community work together. Others might simply enjoy nature together, and transcend their Earthly condition through the sparks of light that are everywhere around.

Others are raising children together, in the spirit of love and oneness. Children are God's stars of light. Through their shared love for the children, the parents or guardians are creating a profound spiritual connection that transcends one's Earthly existence.

When it comes to meditation, my favorite one is to light a candle, hold hands and look into the flame together. After a few minutes, look at one another and telepathically send and receive the most sincere thoughts of gratefulness and the deepest feelings of love.

Of course we are all on a spiritual journey, and the growth process is endless. The more we grow in spirit, the more we accept, respect, and love ourselves, the more we can respect, accept, and love our life partners and everyone else.

In my own experience, once I made a quest for a vision about what it means to make my relationship be a true sacred union. The answer came soon after, during deep meditation, while listening to recorded icaros, surrounded by lit candles and mystical symbols:

The House of God

I accepted my origins
And grew roots deep into the Earth
I became a thick tree with wide branches
And around me grew a house

Beautiful house filled with peace
Yard, sky, stars, open space
And a large lot
With nothing in front

This is the House of God
It has open doors for all of us
There is nothing in front
For God to see who is coming

God has joy and curiosity
Just like me

The elephant with gold on his head
Is stepping into the House of God
And then Lord Shiva comes
I was in deep meditation
Listening to the Shaman's songs on CD
He was invoking Lord Shiva
Thank you, Lord Shiva for coming to me

I didn't know at that time
That the 'elephant' was Lord Ganesha
He is always entering any space first
Before His Father, Lord Shiva

I see my sweetheart on the porch
Contemplating the sky and clouds
He is at peace, and filled with love
And holds a star in his left hand

I'm getting closer to him
We are now holding hands
And sparks of light are coming
Out of our foreheads

There are retreats
In the House of God
And our kids are here
Who doesn't like to hear kids crying
Needs to learn
Respect and love of self

There is a huge table
Made of wood

With food
For the big crowd
That is coming
For healing and learning

There is a terrace
On the top of our house
For all of us to see
The ocean of Love

"Your beloved is fully healed
By the Universe
Through your love
You, Laura must love him
All the time
**Understand and know that
You two are the House of God.**"

What a wonderful vision! I was so very grateful for it! Life, however, sometimes seems to be too far away from spiritual ideals, filled with day-to-day reality, materialism and challenges.

There were times when I had doubts about my relationship, and the fulfillment of this beautiful vision. I didn't let those doubts win, though. Instead, I printed this poem and posted it on our bedroom door. Every challenge we went through, vanished in the presence of these words:

Understand and know that you two are the House of God.

I am now extending this message for all the couples who are reading this book. Be blessed!

The Long Journey

One of my soul-missions is to offer spiritual support to people who are terminally ill or who just passed away. The offering of light is for the purpose of spiritual healing, and to ease soul's journey toward the light.

In *The Tibetan Book of Living and Dying*, Sogyal Rinpoche tells us that the most important gift we can give someone is to help them die at peace. He says that the way we die determines the realm we go to after life, and also the realm in which we will reincarnate in our next existence. There are many rituals for dying in the Tibetan culture; however, not having access to them does not mean that we can't help souls on their long journey. There are simple things, accessible to everyone, that can be used to ease soul's transition toward the light.

Below are a few examples covering different situations I have encountered, revealing priceless soul lessons I was taught by spirit.

Offering of Light for the soul of someone who lived an unhappy life

One of my friends told me about the unexpected death of his mom. It amazed me how, before he actually learned of it, he was in the church, with a lit candle in his hand, and all of a sudden, the candle went out. He also wanted to go out of town that day, but the car kept stopping for no reason, till he understood that was a message from spirit and called his mother's home.

No one answered, so he contacted his sister who went to check on their mom and found her body down on the floor. My friend turned around and drove back home and his car never stopped again...

A few days later, he contacted me and asked me to help with the transition. At night, I got ready, placing his mother's photo on a pillow, in the middle of my copper pyramid, lighted a candle, created a sacred space... but I was so tired, I just wanted to go to sleep. Closing my eyes though, the first image crossing my mind was my friend being so sad and emotional, it woke me up instantly: "Now! Don't wait!"

First I meditated and attuned myself with all Energy Expansion Attunements from Shaman Manin. Little by little I have realized that the shift produced by these attunements opens up the gateway of communication with spirit, so that I can receive messages, see and hear, communicate from the soul.
With a teddy bear in my hands, I prayed and asked Spirit to connect me with my friend's mom for her highest good.

Then I attempted to cut cords, but felt that they were really thick. Almost instantly came a knowing that the cords represented her attachment to unhappiness....
wow... how interesting.... She lived such an unhappy life, she knew nothing else. "Archangel Michael, please cut her cords," I asked... soon, Archangel Michael came to my mind, and with his sword of Light, cut her cords and replaced them with sparkling Divine Light. Right away, my friend's mom now looked released. I'd never seen this woman and didn't have a clue how she looked... it was more of a deep knowing than a clear picture.

Little by little, I've learned to accept these messages, even though very unclear, and validate them as being the truth, rather than disqualify them. For that I'm especially thankful to Sonia Choquette's teachings.

In time, I got so many confirmations that what could have been something I made up, was actually very relevant and made perfect sense to the person related with the story. So, my friend's mom now looked relieved. It was as though a veil was removed from her, allowing her to see and feel in a totally different way. Next, the woman's spirit was telling her son: "Please forgive me, I was an unhappy person my whole life." Later on I understood that she said "forgive me" because her unhappiness made her reject her son's love for years, only to maintain itself.

Now that she was freed of her attachment to unhappiness, she was able to see the love of God....

Next, I passed her a Reiki Attunement, and she enjoyed it and giggled like a child. I was sleepy and doubted my magnetic force that I thought was necessary for this kind of spiritual work... but to my surprise, things were moving forward anyway, and I realized that only my intent of being a vessel, a tool, a channel, mattered – the rest was done by Spirit, through me. The power of my intent, however, was born from spiritual love, from caring deeply about my spiritual friend.

I continued with the White Cross Attunement (picture at the end of this chapter). A white tulip came toward my friend.

Good sign, but yet, I hadn't seen his mom going toward the Light, and wondered if I missed the visualization of her being lifted up. So I asked her soul: "Are you still here?" and she answered right away, "Yes, nobody came to take me, but I'm glad, because I want to stay with my kids a little bit longer."

I understood that she had just discovered the joy and the depth of her love for them, and wanted to live what she'd missed throughout her life.... However, I felt the session was incomplete, and asked Jesus for help. In the next moment, I saw a hand of Light pouring Light on her, then Jesus revealed Himself fully, placed a hand on her shoulder and told her, "You can Love your children even more from the Light. Come with me!"
Holding hands, they went up through clouds and gates, and disappeared in the Light.
God, bless her heart! Thank you, Thank you, and Thank you!

*

Offering of Light for the soul of someone who committed suicide

It took me a while to start. I grew up being taught that suicide is the supreme sin – refusing God's gift for you – the life He gave you. I never reconsidered this till the night when I was told that a friend of a friend committed suicide. Long ago in the past, they had loved each other. I was willing to assist his soul on his journey to the Light, but the old barriers were talking loudly: "What if I interfere with his Karma?" "God, do you allow me to do this?" "God, please help me. God, please forgive him."

I felt empathy with my friend, and imagined how I would go through the death of each man that I ever loved and felt indescribable grief, love, and sorrow blended together. "I am still attached by togetherness on Earth. It would still hurt me beyond any words, and against what I know – that everything is perfect, the soul is infinite and the true connections are eternal." Waiting for a sign from the Divine, soon I had a vision with Jesus, picking up the lost sheep.

Jesus and the lost sheep – by Soord

"Wow, Jesus, you forgive everyone! You don't leave anyone behind!" O, my God, the vision was so profoundly touching me...Jesus gave me the courage to start, so I called on Him, and asked Him to work through me in the process.

No cords were to be cut. "He cut the cords by committing suicide." Wow! So, suicide helped his soul to learn *detachment*. Oh, my God, how true this is! In an instant, I remembered that Bob, my psychic consultant, told me that I did commit suicide myself, in a past life where I was rich and lost everything, feeling angry, broke, alone. Next, I connected to him through my own experience. "It's so easy to do that, it takes a second of disconnect, of despair; everyone is disconnected at times; each of us could do the same, if it is on our Karmic chart." I was amazed at the depth of my insight.

So, I gave the young man's soul the Reiki Attunement, calling on Jesus. A huge relief followed. "God, did you forgive him?" The very next moment, it occurred to me that even though I committed suicide myself, I'm back to the light, doing this kind of work... and so will this person be in his next incarnations. The inflexible, radical "sin" dogma disappeared for ever. "Now I can serve more; I am humbled and blessed."

The last step – the White Cross attunement: as soon as I was running it, three other light beings – his guides – appeared around him, and then they lifted him up to the light; then, a huge number of white roses fell in his parents' house. A white rose came toward his ex-girlfriend's hand, and she received it smiling, and knowing that in spirit there is peace between them forever.

The next day, as I was sharing this experience with her, she said: "He was broke, had no job, and even though he had a new girlfriend and friends and family who loved him, he must have felt really alone.

"Therefore, there is more connection to one of your past lives than you even knew last night. Wow, we are all so interconnected...and we are all here to help each other even if we don't directly know each other.... I knew that before, but now from this experience I really know it, I've internalized it. It has been shown to me."

*

Whitney Houston's journey to Heaven
This poem is dedicated to our dear singer, Whitney Houston, whom I've always loved and thanked for bringing so much love and light into the world through her amazing songs, beautiful energy, and angelic presence.

Whitney Houston passed away
And it was no way back
So I cried and wiped and cried…
She was so dear, and pure and bright!

About a day or two of pain
I felt that sadness kept me away
From exercising my soul mission
Of helping souls to find their way

So I sat down and lit a candle
And prayed for her with all my heart
I wanted her to be at peace, and humble
And find her way toward the light

In my prayers here she comes
Beautiful Whitney wiping tears
She was so sorry she had passed
And wanted to protect her dears

I told her not to worry
And to accept the offer
Of being raised by Angels
And carried to the Heavens

She didn't want to go
Afraid to leave behind
Her daughter and her mother
Outside her loving sight

I told her not to worry
Once in the light she'll charge
With so much love and light
She'll help them very much

I asked my guides to give her
A Reiki initiation
And help her to receive
The love of All Creation

She heard the love of millions
Whose hearts she blessed through music
Each of her fans was offering
A white rose for her spirit

Soon she was covered under
A huge white roses mountain
And she has grasped the love
Waiting for her in Heaven

After a quiet moment
I see all of a sudden
Beautiful Whitney piercing
The white roses mountain

> Angels were there to carry
> Her soul up to Heaven
> While rising she was singing
> ***"I will always love you"***

After this experience, I found peace with her departure. Then the poem unfolded with ease and joy. God bless Whitney Houston!

*

Offering of Light for the soul of someone who was highly evolved spiritually

A friend's grandmother passed away, and he was sad and emotional. He loved her very much. We were holding hands for a few minutes, in a meditative state, and I prayed for him, for her soul, for their connection, and sent them both the Reiki Energy and Shaman Manin's attunements. I felt that she was there, hugging him. He felt that too.

At some point, a message came to my mind, but surprisingly, in Romanian: "*Te-am ales pe tine; voi fi oricand cu tine*" (I chose you; I'll be with you any time). It was weird to receive this message in Romanian, from a Caribbean woman's spirit who never spoke Romanian in her life; later I realized that the message was sent to me through my own grandmother, Roza, who likes my friend's grandmother, for her evolved soul and the similar connection she has with her grandson, as I have with her. From that point on, many times I've seen our grandmothers together during meditation and prayer.

I also suspect that the two of them together helped me and my husband – of Caribbean descent – to meet within the following seven days.

Next morning, I did my usual ceremony to assist her on her long journey.
Even before I started, deep in my heart I knew that she doesn't need it. So it was just an offering of Light.
Instead of using a teddy bear, I used a statue of an African woman, meditating at a candle. Her spirit liked that, since it represented her heritage.

The first step – cutting cords: there were no cords to be cut; she was fully detached.
The second step – giving her a Reiki Attunement: she received it with pure joy and laughter.
The third step – running the White Cross Attunement: she didn't need to be lifted; she was already lifted, up there in the Light.

She gave me a white rose…. No one else gave me a gift before…. And then, she gave her grandson a white rose too, and then she said, "Please help him connect with me." I accepted with joy to assist her gifted grandson on his spiritual journey. As never before, I knew that she's not going to come back in a human body – this was her last incarnation. What an honor!

Two days later, as I was describing this session to my friend, he confirmed that his grandmother was indeed, spiritually in a very special place. He was relieved to now know that she's going to be with him forever. A new beginning….God, bless her soul!

*

Spiritual joy transcending life and death

Bobby and I met in the last two years of his life. From day one, our bond was very strong. My love and admiration for him are eternal – Bobby was one of the most joyful, loving, peaceful, honest, pure-hearted, and responsible persons I ever met. With people like him we would live in a perfect world.

His name was the magic key to my most joyful and blissful state of mind. He was the father-in-law I always wanted – a great role-model and a great friend. I am so honored and grateful for the short time we shared in this lifetime!

His time came, and by his bed, we, the children said, "I love you, Bobby" and he answered, "I love you too." These were his last words we exchanged in this physical world.

For more than twelve hours, we were praying around him as he was between the two worlds. We anointed him with oils, we did Reiki on him and toward the end, I drew the Reiki symbols on his head. Especially the Master Symbol for spiritual healing, that looks like a spiral, the vortex of life.

Soon after his departure, I offered him a Reiki attunement, a cleansing in the ocean of Light, then the White Cross Attunement. When the White Cross started to spin upwards I heard him saying, "That's cool, man!" and he was lifted into the Light.

During the following forty days, he came to me and my husband many times while we were praying for his soul. The key was to pray with joy, not with sorrow.

In my imagination, once my husband and I were on a boat, spreading lit candles and white roses in the turquoise Caribbean water in his honor; he came from the bottom of the sea with a pearl in his hand and told my husband: "This is your childhood."
Thank you, dear Bobby! We love you forever!

After the forty days had passed, even though we continued to pray for his soul every day, we didn't feel his presence as much. Perhaps he was truly enjoying higher levels in the spirit world.

About eight months later, I was in my hospital bed, the first night after a major abdominal surgery. In the middle of the night, half asleep, with my eyes closed, I saw a tall slim man dressed in white pulling the divider curtain.

I opened my eyes and still saw him. Closed my eyes again, not wanting to lose the vision. I knew he was from the spirit world. "If you are with the light, stay, if you are not, leave now!" I commanded.

He got closer, and then I recognized him: it was Bobby! What joy! He touched my head and drew a spiral on it – the vortex of life.... It was exactly how I touched his head before he died, while he was unconscious, between the two worlds.

What a beautiful confirmation – he knew everything we had done for him!
"Thank you, Bobby," I said.

"Thank *you*, my dear!" he responded, and then suddenly disappeared.

Once more I got evidence that our connection is eternal. The joy and love I feel for Bobby are so pure and profound; perhaps our connection reached perfection in previous lifetimes.

I hadn't called on him for help for the time of my surgery, but perhaps at the subconscious level I wanted him to come visit me. After all, the joy he makes me feel is pure medicine.

The last thing I did before leaving the house for the hospital was to splash water on his framed photo. I gave him life (water) to manifest himself, and he sure did…. Thank you, Angel!

*

These are the kinds of spiritual gifts and blessings that all of us can offer, as we're gathering the necessary tools, becoming vessels of Divine Love and Light.

We are so very blessed! And surprisingly, as you can see in the last story, we can also receive gifts back when we most need help.

There is no better gift we can offer to a dying person than to love them and be conduits of Light for them, to ensure their immediate ascension to the Light.

Here is the White Cross attunement, as a gift from Shaman Manin and Councils, to be used if needed for the purpose of healing grief and helping souls in their transition:

White Cross Attunement

Use it as you are called, for the Highest Good of the dying ones and for the ones left behind. God bless!

Two Worlds in Harmony

This subject is way too complex to be developed enough in one small chapter of a book. Therefore, here you will only find a few key words, or qualities – key attitudes on how to bring harmony into your earthly life, when you are on a clear path of spiritual growth and commitment to a better world. I wrote this chapter also as a reminder for myself, because it's not enough to know the right path; I am, like all of us, on an ongoing journey of the soul.

We all need to develop these qualities. It has been a challenge for me, as well as for so many of my spiritual partners, students, and friends.

Humbleness, Protection, Detachment, Responsibility, Acceptance, Patience, Balance, Unconditional Love, and Faith

***

Humbleness and Self Protection

As I immersed myself deeply in my spiritual development, for a while I forgot how to live in the world. I took the law of attraction to the extreme and thought that there is nothing about me that would attract any harm, because I have no more harm in my heart.

On my desk there was printed one of the most beautiful of Louise Hay's affirmations:

"In the infinity of life where I am, all is perfect, whole and complete. I am divinely protected and guided. All is well in my world." I took *"I am divinely protected"* to the extreme, and thought that nothing bad can happen to me.

With that in mind one day I offered to help a woman who couldn't be trusted and ended up with a big financial loss. I learned that we are responsible to protect ourselves and our goods at all times.

It doesn't matter how spiritual we are, how important is our mission and how sacred are our belongings, our bodies and our sacred objects are still vulnerable in this rough world and they are for us to protect. I had to accept: before asking for Divine protection, I must do my part and not force the Divine's hand. I learned to be humble.

The new affirmations on my desk for the next few months were:

I accept to protect myself.
I accept the material world for what it is and for what it is not.
I keep praying for everyone's time of kindness and purity to come, while keeping myself safe.
I ask, and hear the Divine advice in any situation.
I follow the Divine advice for my highest good and the highest good of all concerned.

Energetic protection is equally important. As we develop our healing capabilities and intuitive capabilities, out of excitement and curiosity we have the tendency to stay open energetically, to perceive, receive, interpret, and give.

In truth, there is a time for everything. We all have to remember to "zip up our jackets" as we are walking through crowds, to protect ourselves, and to only open up fully in safe environments.

One day a friend sent me the following anonymous quote: *"The will of God will never take you where the Grace of God will not protect you."*
My thought: we are protecting ourselves by listening to God within, to our intuition; otherwise our ego might take us in places where God would never take us, in places where we are not protected. Humbleness means considering that we might not know everything, therefore it would be wise to calm down our impulsivity and listen to our intuition.

*

Detachment

At some point I was giving Reiki sessions to patients in a hospital, and one of them was a very sick woman. She was at risk of death, and she had two small children. One evening I went to see her, and found her little daughter curled in her bed, hugging her tight. It touched me so deeply, I became attached to her recovery, and forgot all about respecting the will of God. That night I woke up from an amazing dream where my whole body was exhaling Light toward her, including through my feet!

I never thought about doing such a thing, even though I do pray at night asking God and the Councils of Light to send me in my sleep on missions of healing, which they have been doing pretty often.

Giving even through my feet, in a convulsive, excessive manner was an obvious sign of attachment.

The next day, realizing that my dream was a projection of my attachment, and not a guided distant healing session during sleep, I decided to detach.
My prayers for that sick mother were strong enough to be heard by the Universe. The Universe only needs to hear them once. When we keep asking for the same thing, louder and louder, that means we are attached and we don't have enough faith that God has heard our calling and will do what's for the highest good.

> *Above the clouds it is always sunny*
> *Under the clouds it is rainy or dark*
> *Fly above the clouds and you will see*
> *The beauty and infinity of life*

*

Responsibility

"If you are indulging in anxiety, fear and worry, it is a waste of energy. Take responsibility for your decisions, look at your actions and think forward. Fear is false evidence appearing real. It could be a way to avoid reality. Failure is expected. Self-sabotaging behavior and excuses are running the show. Face everything and rejoice. Focus your energy and relax." – Shaman Manin

Sometimes being willing to live in the moment is possible only if we fully accept our suffering. Resistance to reality leads to the desire to escape the present moment.

Only when we become able to embrace pain and be grateful for the opportunities of growth that it is presenting to us, can we love the present moment no matter what. We are responsible for our happiness.

The same applies for the people we love: we should not indulge in anxiety about their issues either, but rather trust their higher self, their guidance, their destiny and our Creator, and just keep praying and having good expectations.

Be easy on yourself. That doesn't mean being lazy or dropping responsibilities; it could mean dropping resistance against responsibilities. It could also mean knowing when to stop serving others, to rest and to regain personal balance and well being.
We are responsible for keeping ourselves in good shape. A friend told me once: "Stay blessed and bright. Many people depend on your light." That was a good reminder for me, to rest more.

*

Acceptance for where each of us is

It's a journey to really learn tolerance and compassion sometimes. I guess the first step is to stop thinking that life should be a bed of roses and accept the pain involved in growth and transformation. We need so much Divine mercy, forgiveness, love, and grace in the process. God, help us all!

Accept people for where they are in their awakening process. Rather than being disappointed, be grateful that you have already learned the lessons they have not yet learned, and pray for their time to come.

"If you want to awaken all of humanity, then awaken all of yourself. If you want to eliminate the suffering in the world, then eliminate all that is dark and negative in yourself. Truly, the greatest gift you have to give is that of your own self-transformation." – Lao Tzu

Indeed it takes deep transformation to grow and then not suffer when you look around at people who are making self-destructive choices. It takes a lot to accept their path with peace, to just give love and pray for their time to come. It takes a lot to not get pulled down by the feet. Only when we surrender to God we can succeed.

*

Patience

Where are you rushing? You are running so fast after happiness, love, bliss, fulfillment, growth, and achievement, and you think that others are dragging you down by the feet? But what happiness could you experience by yourself, if others are left behind?

Be patient! Accept your role of being a teacher, a healer, a support person. You are privileged.

Be patient! In the infinity of life, time is irrelevant. So you can't waste your time or your life. It's not a waste.

The growth process will never end for anyone. Growing together is more important than anything. And after all, patience might be your lesson.

This is how I had to talk to myself many times....

*

Balance – all areas of life are equally important

Don't refuse any part of you. You are perfect from A to Z. No part is better than another.

The seven chakras and their functions are equally important and we need to honor all of them for a Godlike life. Same with our duties and responsibilities: the earthly ones such as maintaining enough financial stability, at least for our homes and modest living, should not be considered less important than our spiritual ones. They are all connected.

In terms of occupation, as long as we don't harm anyone through our jobs, we need to honor our jobs and put as much good energy in them as possible. Good energy matters whether we practice healing arts or not. Wherever we are, we breathe out love, and we make a difference. A law professor told me once, "Any organization would be happy just to have you in the building." I was doing a good job as IT Coordinator, but my most important contribution was to be a cheerleader and to give a smile or a Reiki session to my co-workers as each of them was going through life challenges.

Honor all professions and all talents. If you are on a spiritual path but you also have a profession that doesn't directly involve healing arts and spiritual growth, honor it. You are honoring that talent of yours and you gain balance. Prepare for change, but don't force the hand of the Divine. If one day the Divine wants you to only practice healing arts, it will show you the way without any struggle. Everything will unfold with ease and bliss. Meanwhile you must maintain your own balance and honor your other ways of giving to the world.

We have to find our way up, and our way down. True ascension is when we can go up and down as we wish and as necessary. The two worlds are one, at least for as long as our souls are connected with Planet Earth.

Our spiritual life is an awakened way of living life; we gain eternal transformation in the direction of our new spiritual realizations as we apply them in all areas of our life.

We have to learn balance. Some people are too much into the physicality and materialism, others are too much into spirit, and they think life on Earth is nonsense. In truth, we all made a choice to come into our bodies. It wasn't time yet for us to be free spirits.

We can't judge God or the Universe for the way these laws are created. If we can accept the suffering and embrace the joy of being embodied, we won't resist the lessons we still have to learn.

Transformation takes time. It's like a tree... it needs so many years to grow strong and stable.

This is why it is so important to accept ourselves for who we are and where we are in the process at any given time, and just keep going...all that matters is our intent and commitment to grow.

*

Unconditional Love

Remember that unhappy people just didn't get enough love. If they make you miserable, they are actually asking for love and compassion. If they were happy they wouldn't do that to you, they wouldn't do that to themselves.

At some point I was struggling in my acceptance and love toward a woman who was very hard to deal with. One night, I meditated and prayed before going to sleep, asking for guidance, and then I had an amazing dream. First I heard:

> "All I want from you is to see compassion
> Just give love to this demanding woman
> Till her cup is full
> Her cup of love will overflow and
> She will become a teacher."

Then, I saw that woman, in her regular pathetic appearance. Listening to the guidance, I sent her healing in my sleep. I took her on a journey to a beautiful beach, and showed her peace, joy, and love. I took her to the roots of her childhood and told her that life is so simple, and that God loves her.

A few nights later, she came in my dream in a very empowering state of mind, as I never saw her in real life. She was all sparkling and full of love and wisdom, and she taught me important things for my own life. Even though in daily life the change was not stunning, in spirit, she did receive the blessings and she did become a teacher.
A few months later she had a stroke. Despite everyone's expectations, she survived. I knew that spirit knew… and helped me find love in my heart for her before she might have left this planet. Completion is priceless. Love is the way and the best medicine.

Even in very difficult encounters, send
LOVE – FORGIVENESS – PEACE.
This is what Shaman Manin taught me.

It's so powerful; it can even make the angel of death step back. In spirit, everyone knows that the greatest power in the world is the power of love.

"Only from the heart can you reach the sky" – Rumi

You are love, but how do you give love and be understood? Whatever way we manifest our love for people needs to be suitable for their paradigm.

Speak in the "language" of your audience. People don't care that you went around the world and learned other languages. If you can't speak in their language of understanding, they won't get the treasures you want to bring back to them.

When it seems complicated, go to the basics and remember, we are all related through the grace of love. Don't fall into judgment or sorrow – just love from the center of your heart. Remember, even the "ugly" caterpillars will, one day, become beautiful butterflies.

*

Faith

To have faith means to know we are not alone.
To have faith means to be willing to listen.
To have faith means to be willing to see the truth.
To have faith means to put aside our rational, linear thinking and surrender to the possibility of miracles.
To have faith means to put no barriers in the way of the Divine manifestations.
To have faith means to be focused on spirit.

The Divine is everywhere. The Divine loves us so deeply and unconditionally, we can't even imagine. Our relationship with the Divine can make us feel whole and complete no matter what.

"Know me, Laura!
You must believe I love you!"

When I heard those words, in deep meditation, tears were falling down my face… the words came with such a high vibration of love, they made my whole body shift into sparkles of light, and I realized that to be focused on spirit means to be focused on God's love for us.

This love also comes through all God's messengers and through all creation. Loving our Spiritual Masters, the Angels, the Spiritual Guides, all people, animals, plants, waters, our Mother Earth, our friends from the other side, the stars and the whole Universe, means loving God, and through the mirror of love, means accepting God's love.

*

How can we maintain these qualities? Our mind can make us or break us. Our thoughts are powerful, so it is important to see life from a positive perspective.

However, easy to say – if we don't make a sustained effort to keep our vibration high, our mind will only create and entertain illusions, and the biggest of all is the illusion of unhappiness, rooted in the loneliness of separation from the Source.

In the effort to keep ourselves in a high vibration, in the next chapter you will find a few tips on how to stay focused on spirit – focused on light.

How can we stay Focused on Spirit?

To be focused on spirit means to be connected with our divine spark, to be connected with the Creator, and to ask spirit for guidance, inspiration, healing, and teachings, for our highest good and the highest good of all.

God, please bless us and help us see and hear your love.

This is my deepest desire. If we would all hear and see God's love for us, we would never feel miserable. We would live in peace; we would know who we really are; we would know how much we are loved; we would know that all is well.

Keeping our vibration high is essential. The spiritual tools below can help anyone in the attempt to be present. Only when we are present, when we are free of the turmoil of a distracted or troubled mind, can we be focused on spirit. When the noise of our minds is loud, the gentle intuitive voice cannot be heard.

This is not a complete list of tools, but rather a list of tools that I have used so far, tools that helped me live the content of this book. They have all proven their beauty, their power, their merit in helping me and many others attain the connection with the Universal Consciousness, receive divine inspiration, grow spiritually, and serve humanity more and more.

"If you really want to walk this spiritual path, you need to concentrate every day. You need to focus your mind. It doesn't matter how you choose to do it. You want to do it through prayer, do it through prayer. You prefer meditation, that's okay, too. You prefer mantra, that is good. You prefer singing, that is perfect. It doesn't matter which way you choose. Each one of us, according to our qualities, according to our habits, according to our tendencies, will receive more benefits from one way or from another. What is important is that your mind gets concentrated." Don Diego

As you read through, ask yourself which ones of these ways to focus are most appealing to you. Feel free to use any or all of them, to combine them, and to add any new elements you might find to your own list.

***

Awareness of the senses and awareness of one's body

Honor your body, the temple of your spirit. Love yourself and know that you are an instrument for miracles.

As you smell, taste, see, touch, and hear, pay attention and notice how you feel, put in words the sensations, impressions, little things that will help you recognize better the language of your own body.

Make your space a sacred temple. Your space is where you should be able to fully open to receive from the Divine. Sacred objects, spiritual icons, crystals, candles, souvenirs, small musical instruments, essential oils, sage – all of these are wonderful ceremonial tools.

Bodywork: receive massage, Reiki, acupuncture, or other treatments that help body-mind-spirit to get into a state of balance.

Listen to relaxation music and/or icaros – songs for healing.

Listen to and/or practice drumming. The rhythm of the African or Native American drumming or any other indigenous drumming is the rhythm of life, is a gateway to a trance-like state of mind. Drumming activates the right side of the brain; it awakens the intuition, the healer within, the knowing that we are all one.

Practice chakra meditation: visualize the seven colors – the seven vortexes of light in your body. From the bottom toward the top: red, orange, yellow, green, blue, purple, and white. (See my first book, *The Journey of the Colorful Stars*)

Design by John (Ion) Dragutescu

Practice Yoga – it helps you get your body functioning properly and it opens all your chakras and prepares you for deep meditation. If you don't have time to take full 90-minute yoga classes, at least practice the Sun Salutation at your own convenience. It only takes about 20 minutes. The entire sequence is available on the internet.

*

Connecting with nature and animals, and finding communion with all creation

The simplicity and purity of nature and animals brings us back to a state of balance, gratitude, communion with all creation.

The forest, the garden of flowers, fruits, and vegetables, the sea and the sand, the mountains and the lakes, the clouds passing by… the cuteness, innocence and beauty of all baby animals…

When I see any of these beautiful gifts of our Creator, even in electronic format on my computer, I immerse into the ocean of love for life.

Visiting sacred spots – temples, energy vortexes is always an empowering experience. We always come back charged with energy, inspired to connect more often with the infinity of vibrant love of the Universe.

*

Communion with the four elements during meditation:

–Water: Take long showers under a "waterfall of light" (see my first book, *The Journey of the Colorful Stars*); put your feet in warm water with salt – one of the most relaxing and detoxifying experiences.
–Fire: Practice candle meditation (see *The Journey of the Colorful Stars*).
–Air: Use essential oils, sage and incense sticks during meditation.
–Earth: Practice meditation with crystals (see *The Journey of the Colorful Stars*).

The communion with the four elements brings us closer to the divine. Merging into the simplicity and purity of life, we can let go of all our thoughts and turn our eyes and ears toward Spirit.

*

Group or couple meditation

When we meditate together, an invisible fluid of light is being emanated and shared between the meditation partners. The spiritual connection between the meditation partners can become strong enough to function as a web of light. It happened to me often to receive intuitive messages urging me to pray for a particular individual I only met once in group meditation. Long lasting friendships are being developed through this practice. The immediate benefit of group meditation is a tremendous sense of oneness, wholeness, comfort, and peace.

When a couple meditates together, they give light and strength to their silver cord – the spiritual connection that makes their relationship profound, more loving, and meaningful. I believe these connections are transcending lifetimes – these meditation sessions are creating such a powerful magnet between the two, they will meet again to share and enhance even more their sacred union.

*

Communion with the Divine

Pure Love for the Divine is the way to live a happy, focused on spirit life.

Through our prayers, faith, and concentration on the holiness of our spiritual Masters, we can reach the highest vibrational frequencies. Some of us pray in silence; some use mantras or chanting.

In that state of oneness and bliss, when we pray, we talk to the Divine. When we meditate, we listen to the Divine. Take time at the end of your prayers to listen, and transform the monolog into a dialog – a very spiritual one.

Prayer and meditation, focusing on the Divine, is powerful when done individually, as well as in groups. Each way has its own purpose.

Spiritual Retreats are also very empowering.

How wonderful it is to watch the stars, the galaxies together as a group of spiritual friends, and to share the stillness, or the sacred movements of yoga, or the sacred teachings of the gurus or the shamans!

*

Invocations and Energetic Expansion Attunements

My teacher, Shaman Manin, has been receiving many spiritual gifts from the Councils and gracefully shared them for our highest good. These gifts are meant to raise our vibration and to help us become vessels for healing and teaching.

We can raise our vibration by visualizing the images below and by practicing the mantras associated with them on a daily basis.

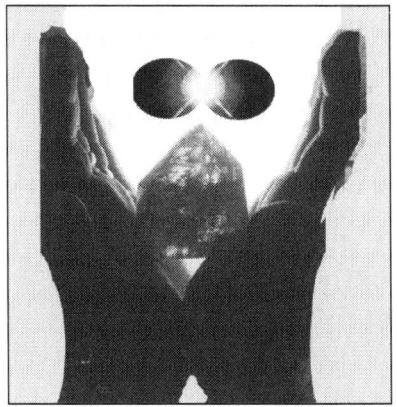

SoDalited Attunement

I am SoDalited to receive all the blessings that God and the whole Universe have to give me!

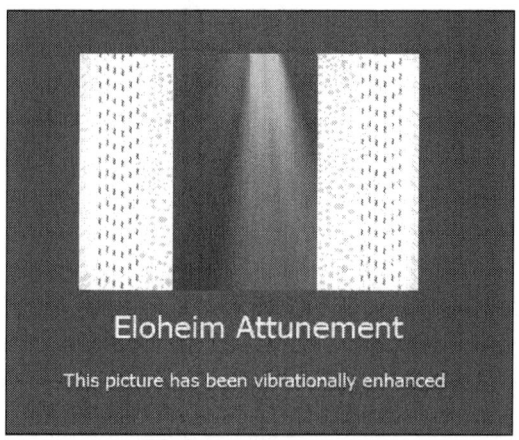

Eloheim Attunenent

I am welcoming God in my life, and all His Councils of
Light,
Healers, teachers, guardian angels
To guide me
And protect me
And heal me
And teach me
And talk through me
And write through me
And heal through me
And teach though me
For my highest good
And the highest good of all

*(Note: please customize this invocation to reflect your
guides and your desire; usually I am calling on Jesus
Christ, Lord Shiva, Buddha, Native American guides,
Reiki guides, Archangels Michael, Raphael, Gabriel and
Uriel. I am also calling on the spirits of my grandmothers
and my first esoteric teacher, Alexandru)*

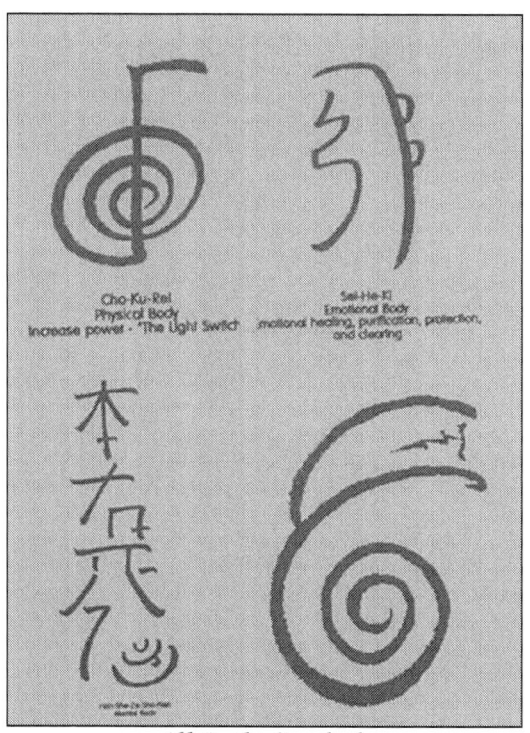

All Reiki Symbols

Then, drawing the Reiki Symbols on your palms: I'm bringing in the Reiki Energy to heal me and heal through me any physical diseases, emotional wounds and attachments, old mental patterns and spiritual debts and blockages, till I am fully healed, shining from within.

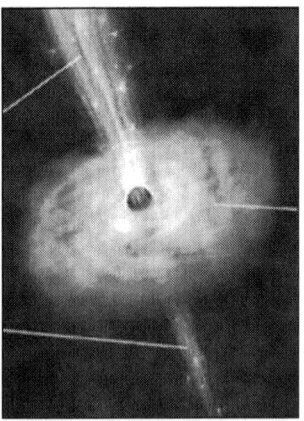

Cleansing-Healing Thought Form Attunement

Then, looking at the image that represents the "Cleansing-Healing Thought Form Attunement," I am breathing in and out three times, inhaling Light spiraling through the top of my head, clockwise, and exhaling all stress and negativity in the opposite direction.

Santara-Cusgal Attunement

Then, I am looking in the center of the image above, breathing in and out through my crown chakra.

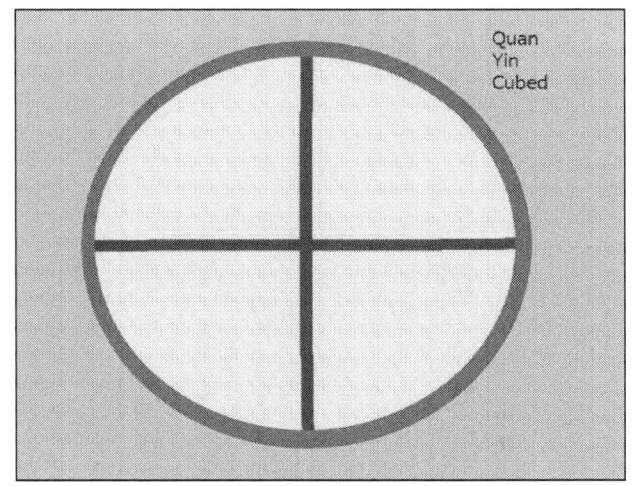

Quan Yin Cubed Attunement

Then, looking at the image representing a circle, and placing my right hand on my heart, I say:
I am running the Quan-Yin-Cubed Attunement on my heart
For forgiveness, mercy, peace, grace, and compassion

Shaman Manin says:

I love myself. I forgive myself. I am at peace with myself.

I love you, I forgive you. I am at peace with you.

Aho.

(*Note: "You" means anyone*)
And we can go further and say:
I love the whole world.
I forgive everyone who has hurt me in the past.

I am at peace with all that is.

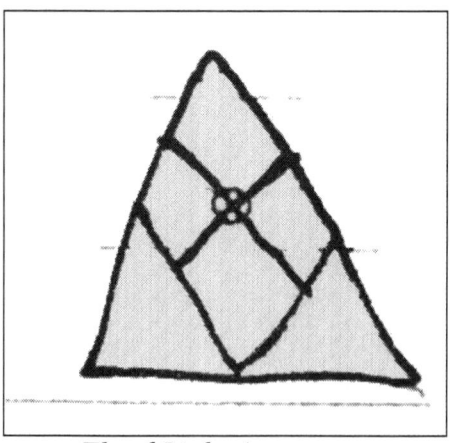

Flood Light Attunement

Then, I look at the yellow triangle, representing the Flood Light Attunement, saying
"Run Flood Light!"

Then, look at the image below, and say "Run DNA expansion attunement."

Then, say "Run 11.11K for my cosmic, monadic, athmic, buddhic, mental, emotional and etheric body. Run 11.11K for my crown, third eye, throat, heart, solar plexus, sacral, and root. Run 11.11K for my highest good, for each cell of my body."

"Focus as long as possible on highly vibrational things," Manin said.

When Shaman Manin shared these energies with me, in the beginning I felt overwhelmed, wondering when in the world I was going to do all this. But then it occurred to me that I was still spending time thinking useless thoughts, which can be replaced with powerful thoughts such as running these energies. That's very important – *to keep ourselves busy with what really supports us on our spiritual journey, to feed the Light Within, and create new patterns of thought and emotion.*

We are creatures of habit, and little by little I understood that *being happy and joyful is a habit* just as it is to be sad, worried or depressed. It takes work, it takes time, but it's worth doing.

> *"If humans live and maintain this state of balance and love, imagine the possibilities!"* – Shaman Manin

*

Dreams

Going to bed with the intent of being protected and guided, avoiding a heavy meal before going to bed, taking a warm shower, cleansing the energy with sage or essential oils, practicing invocations and prayers would cleanse energetically and would help with having better dreams.

The more we raise our vibration, the more quality dreams we will have.

Writing the dreams down just the way they were is very important. Often the dreams are coded, wrapped up in a metaphor and symbolism that is hard to understand. Just write them down without modifying them, and your interpretation is also important to be noted, but not instead of the raw dream, rather beside the raw dream.

When the dreams are truly infused with divine inspiration, we feel different – our vibration is higher.

Whatever we don't remember has still been captured by our subconscious mind, and will serve us when we really need that inspiration.

In this book, I have shared many beautiful messages that I have received during sleep. I would dare to say that going to sleep with the intent of channeling healing and Universal Consciousness has been my greatest asset. When we are relaxed, when we travel through the Universe, we can do so many things that we are normally blocking while awake.

To me dreams are the evidence that we are all able to have amazing spiritual experiences, if we can only step aside from the heavy armor of our minds.

*

Single pointed meditations; the importance of the tears

These meditation techniques have been my first key to strength of spirit, inspiration, peace through emptiness of thought, intuition, and spiritual growth.

My teacher, Alexandru, taught me these two meditation techniques when I was 19. He asked me not to share them with anyone, so I kept them a secret for many years. However, seeing their tremendous positive impact in my life, I really wanted to share them with everyone who is interested in meditation practices and spiritual growth.

We now live in different times, when sacred teachings are not a secret anymore. We are now living in an era of abundant sharing. However, I still waited till I had received my teacher's consent from the spirit world before sharing these techniques.

For more information about Alexandru and my story as a beginner of these techniques, read my first book, *The Journey of the Colorful Stars*.

When focusing our eyes on one point, our mind starts to focus more and more on one thought. Where our thought goes, our energy flows.

Therefore, if you decide to try practicing this meditation technique, make sure you only entertain positive thoughts during meditation. Otherwise it could be as destructive as poison.

When focusing our eyes on one point, our physical eyes align with our third eye. When practiced on a regular basis, the techniques can lead to the gradual opening of the third eye. They also stimulate the pituitary gland, which is the master gland, determining the good functionality of all endocrine glands in the body.

If you choose to practice these techniques, do it only when you are in very good health, and especially when you are in a very good emotional and mental state. Otherwise, just pray and practice candle meditation – look into the flame of a candle.

Also, before practicing these techniques, practice the invocations above, and call in your spiritual guidance to protect you and guide you. Do not open doors and do not play with unseen forces you cannot control, without any protection. You are responsible for your well-being at all times.

Technique No. 1
Place a dot on the wall, and sit comfortably on a chair or pillow, with your spine straight. Look only at the dot, right in front of you, at a level a little bit higher than your eye level. Do not blink.
Your eyes will produce tears. The urge to blink will be overwhelming. Sometimes tears will fall down your face, sometimes they will not.

This meditation should be practiced only for a few minutes. If the tears are falling, that meditation session reached its best result – through the tears, all stress hormones are being cleansed away, the parasympathetic system is activated, lowering heart rate and breathing, and pain-killing hormones are being released. Don't wipe the tears, let them dry and wash your face at the end of your meditation session.

After a few minutes of open eyes meditation, close your eyes and continue to meditate for another 10 -15 minutes. If tears were falling while you had your eyes opened, perhaps you will find yourself in an incredible state of peace and liberating emptiness of thoughts. Just breathe and be. This is a great state in which you can receive inspiration, messages from the other side, and spiritual healing.

As you practice this technique, your magnetism – your energy – expands. You might see a circle of light flickering around the dot in the beginning. If you practice on a regular basis, after a few minutes that circle of light can expand as much as a few feet in each direction. That expansion you see on the wall is a mirror of your expanded energy.
Perhaps this is a very clear explanation of the first poem I wrote in this book.

Technique No. 2
Use a makeup pencil and make a dot on your forehead, between your eyebrows. Sit comfortably and look in the mirror, basically practicing the exact meditation as above – except, now you are focusing inward, not outward.

If practiced on a regular basis, this technique can help you see your own aura in the mirror, while your eyes are fixed only on the dot.

Alternate the two techniques, and create unity between your outward and inward worlds. They are one.

Again, it is your responsibility to protect yourself, and only practice these techniques as described above. If anything unusual happens, stop the meditation session immediately. Even though I am sharing these precious, simple, and powerful techniques with you, I still encourage you to find a teacher of your own, who will customize a technique more suitable just for you, who will protect you and guide you in your spiritual journey.

*

Being of service

When the healing energy flows, Universal Consciousness flows. It is unlimited, infinite and eternal. It is bliss.

Reiki Sessions and Reiki Initiations have been a really amazing way for me to stay focused on spirit.

You already read many Reiki stories and the wonderful spiritual messages received, throughout this book. I also encourage you to read my book entitled *Reiki and the Path to Enlightenment*, and nevertheless, to take the Reiki classes and receive the Reiki initiations.

Shamanic work is more expanded spiritual and vibrational healing work.

It can include Reiki or other hands-on healing modalities, as well as working with crystals, oils, plants, prayers, universal energies. It is a fascinating, enlightening, and rewarding work. If you feel the calling, find a teacher and go on this path with an open heart and mind.

*

Sacred Ceremonies

There are many kinds of Sacred Ceremonies, led by Shamans of different cultures.
Many of them are available only in close circles, or for people who have been on a spiritual path for a while. It takes preparation to be able to participate in these ceremonies, so that participants can be opened enough, and ready to focus on the essence, on the spiritual depth of the experience, rather than be immersed in the fascination of the Shamanic Practices.

Once you are on a spiritual path and you have a teacher, you will find the right ceremonies to attend; you will be ready to immerse yourself in the most profound explorations of the soul.

My experience started with Solstice Ceremonies led by Shaman Manin, as well as Native American Powwows and Sweat lodges. They helped me cleanse, reconnect, let go, and find the deepest peace and rejuvenation.

In the chapter below I am sharing my experiences during my participation in the Sacred Plant Ceremonies led by Don Diego of Sachavacay.

Part IV

Shamanic Sacred Ceremonies

At some point in my spiritual journey, I felt called to participate in a Sacred Plant Shamanic Ceremony, and allow myself to access the deepest corners of my subconscious mind, while being led, guided and protected by a powerful Shaman of the ancient Peru. This profound experience is not advisable unless one attains a certain level of spiritual development, and while being in good emotional and physical health. It is also a must having such experience only under the guidance of a true Master Shaman, and only with the highest intent of spiritual growth.

I followed the Shaman's advice and prepared well by being on a diet, meditating, and focusing on my intent for a week before the ceremony.

To experience *oneness*, the Shaman taught us to surrender. He also told us to *focus*. To me, *surrender* and *focus* are the opposite, how can I do both? The answer was given: *Sit with your spine straight, focus on your breathing and on my song – the icaros, and surrender to the Divine will.*

Surrender… easy to say; I've tried before, in vain. In the past, my controlling mechanism had been always winning. In the meantime, though, my ego became more obedient, through detachment, faith, and humbleness.

A sacred Shamanic ceremony is meant to help participants attain a pure connection with our essence, our spark of light within. In this process, we can learn who we really are; we can learn how to die, and how to live a better life.

As the Shaman said, when we die, we only take with us our spiritual growth. In the face of death, nothing else is important. We were participating in the sacred ceremony for the purpose of spiritual growth.

Stanislav Grof, one of the founders of Transpersonal Psychology, says that the symbolic meeting with the moment of death leads to a spiritual opening, a mystical experience. The ego dies, and a spiritual and transpersonal identity develops. Then, we can identify with nature, animals, plants, the universe… everything. As a result we have more racial, cultural, political, and religious tolerance.

The Sacred Plant Shamanic Ceremony definitely reached this purpose and way more. I give thanks to Shaman Diego, to my teacher, Shaman Manin, who prepared me for that moment, to my spiritual guide Alexandru and ultimately, to the Divine.

The realization described below is not to be learned by reading. My sharing is only an act of service through passing on knowledge and inspiration. Only experiencing, one can have his/her personal realization.

Also, everyone is experiencing what their soul needs at the moment; for me, the experience seemed to be a mirror of the deepest level of where I was at that moment on my spiritual journey. The essence of all teachings along my journey to that point was summarized, reinforced, and empowered. The possibilities became reality at the spiritual level.

Note: Jesus is my Spiritual Master Guide; to relate with my experience, think about your own Master Guide if you believe in one. The Master Guide you have faith in, is *the one, for you.*

*

Transcending Ego

The group formed a circle and the Shaman started with a blessing. Everyone drank the Sacred Plant. The Shaman drank it too, and then he started to sing icaros – songs for healing.

I was in meditation posture, calling on my teacher, Alexandru. My breathing was tranquil. About 45 minutes later, I started to feel my chakras spinning, from the top toward the bottom: crown, third eye, throat, heart, then hands, then solar plexus, sacral, feet.

I wasn't afraid of the unknown, knowing that I am protected. A while ago I had learned that my first Guardian Angel is my pure heart.

In spirit, my teacher Alexandru came for me. "Look in my eyes," I heard his voice in my heart. "Focus, fetito." (*fetito* means little girl in Romanian).
Focus on Jesus! – I thought.
Jesus! I called, and saw Jesus in front of me; he was not well defined, and grey.

Even though I had my mouth closed, energetically my mouth opened and I started to throw up energetically. I was purging old emotional traumas.

I wanted to open my eyes but the hood covered them so I saw deep dark.
"Jesus!" I called.
"Look for the Light in your heart," I thought.

Instantly I understood my grandmother Mama Nana who was blind for the last four years of her life, and I started to practice what I taught her – to look inside for the Light.

I took my hood away and looked at the Shaman. I was humbled by the power of his hypnotic eyes. I was in trance, almost numb.

"Jesus!" I called.
Jesus was in front of me, and he was *Jesus, the Gray*. This was an analogy with Gandalf, the Wizard, in the movie *Lord of the Rings*: he was gray and then "upgraded" to white. Jesus in front of me was the projection of my faith in Jesus. So at that moment, it was gray.

In my trance-like experience, my body started to vanish, till I had nothing left of it but two points: my mind and my heart.
"Focus, fetito!" – My teacher's voice came from deep in my heart
"Jesus!" I called again.

People around were making different noises, and it brought me back for a second, and I felt again my body, numb, and got bombarded with all the negativity that was released by them. Also, the person next to me moved his blanket which touched my knee. The memory of the guys who tried to rape me when I was a sophomore in high school, after they got me drunk enough to lose control, came back to my mind.

That was the experience which, through the years, stopped me from letting go of the controlling mechanism; I wanted to face that, and my participation in this ceremony was the ultimate proof of my commitment to do so.

"Focus, fetito!" I heard again.
"Jesus!" I called again.

At the energetic level, I was purging more deep emotional traumas, old things from forgotten times, maybe hundreds of lifetimes ago. After a while, it stopped, and I was able to fully focus on my luminous body's experience.

In my trance-like experience, my body dissolved again and became two points – mind and heart. I wanted the whole experience of a free spirit: to download my mind into my heart, and then be just one point – the free spirit, the Heart of Light. I accepted to let go fully.

"What if I'm not going to come back from this deep trance?" I asked myself. "I'm ready for anything God wants me to experience; I am not afraid and now accept to let go of my mind, and fully surrender." That was a huge breakthrough since it was the first time in my life when I accepted to be led in an altered state of consciousness.

"My soul is eternal; however, what if I'm not coming back, and didn't say Goodbye to my parents?"
I gave my mom a hug; she was like a little girl in my arms. Then, I kissed my father's hand, and put my heart at his feet.

Then, I gave a big, loving hug to my Romanian friend, Geny. "If my parents didn't receive my message, I know you are receiving it, you'll know the truth."

All images were kind of gray and not very well defined. I was distracted again by others around me and came back into my body for a second.

"Focus, fetito!" I heard again.
"Jesus!" I called again.

Then, all of a sudden, a breathing technique that I've never been taught in this life took me over. It felt like I'm breathing through my crown and while exhaling, I'm downloading my entire mind into my heart.
Yogi, I am one with a Yogi!
A yogi that perhaps was me in a previous life woke up in me. Lord Shiva was standing in front of me, as a shape made of light, in a meditative posture.

"I am now a Yogi!" I thought.
Shiva consciousness awakened in me.
Shiva's statue made of Light was right in front of me.
Meditative trance. Bliss. Void.

I was disturbed again by surroundings and everything vanished.
"Jesus!" I called again, wanting the deepest spiritual experience.
Jesus came back, replacing the image of the Yogi.
Breathing deeply, I felt how I was vanishing again.

"Jesus!" I called again.

"If I'm not going to have anything (body, mind, and ability to hold), the only way to have Jesus is to *be* Jesus," I thought.

"*I am one with Jesus!*" I told myself
He was gray, in front of me, but then He jumped into me, dissolved all of me, and I became *one* with Jesus.

"*I am one with Jesus!*" This time it wasn't an affirmation, it was my reality.
I was on a huge cross, gray, with a crown of thorns on my head. I had no pain.
Jesus consciousness awakened in me.
"Jesus had no pain, He was already pure spirit on the cross!" – I observed.

"I am one with Jesus!" I heard… and affirmed, at the same time.
"Now, since I am one with Jesus, I can look for God."

"God!!!" I called.
I was one with Jesus, flying through space, clouds, Universe, looking for God, while breathing out my soul.
Everything was still gray, no colors.
In that moment, the Shaman came in front of me and said: "Stop! Focus your mind!"

I was fully back in my body again, looked at the Shaman and saw the strength of his spirit, and listened to him without arguing, despite my initial desire to let go of my mind and just be my heart, free spirit.

Something clicked in me:

"Don Diego reads our minds, he is a true healer, he has all spiritual gifts opened, and he's able to take care of all of us even though he drank the Sacred Plant, just like us; he didn't let go of his mind, he is *mastering* his mind! Just like my teacher Alexandru taught me to do too – 'Fetito, when you'll master your mind, you'll master everything.' "
I admired him profoundly.

"Focus, fetito!" – my teacher Alexandru said again. The last arguing moment consumed: "But I've learned that when you *are* Light, you don't have to *focus on* Light…however, Jesus wants me to be in this body, and use my mind and my heart together. Being only the heart is the ultimate experience. Now I've been incarnated, have received the gift and the responsibility to be in a body, on Earth, and serve. So be it!"

In that moment, I saw a Holy Cross of Light forming in me, from the crown to the heart and from one shoulder to another.
"I am the Cross of Light!"
In my teenage years, I had a dream about the Spiritually Guided Life Force Energy, in the form of billions of colorful stars coming down in a spiral that entered in a huge holy cross. Through the years, my interpretation took the following shape – "Healing comes through Faith; Reiki is my destiny."

Now, I am the cross, I am one with Jesus, or in other words, I am my faith.
The spiral of spiritually guided Life Force Energy comes now directly through me.

A shift occurred. I learned how to give up my ego, and let my spirit lead. All resistance disappeared.

Silence… Awakening… Understanding… "I wasn't really surrendering; I was thinking through the process way too much and tried to control my experience."

So I took a really deep and peaceful breath, and surrendered.

I was alive, but had the experience of a free spirit. In the next moment, my luminous body was dancing in the room. Then I was pouring Light on the head of each person around me who was working their way through. In spirit, I was in service.

It was easy to move my body. I was fully in my body, but at the same time, fully aware of my spirit.
Now the second distinct part of my experience started.

*

I sat down in a lotus posture, my hands in a prayer position, right in front of my heart, and started to breathe in a brand new way. I was in total peace.
Buddha consciousness awakened in me.

Next, I saw Jesus again, right in front of me. He was now *Jesus, the White*! That meant to me that my highest faith in Jesus was attained.

Next, I was distracted by people around. That made it possible for some negative energy to try to enter in my sacred space, like huge, pink-red skinless fingers. I cut them and replaced everything with Divine Light.

I have learned my power of turning demons into angels.

Then, my body was alert, but my luminous body was in front of Jesus again. My body was the observer. Jesus blessed me and placed a round white crown of light on my head. I was made of shiny white light and saw myself in the future replacing my outfits in the closet from colorful to white.

Then, the bliss started. It was all experienced through my connection with the souls and people that I visited for the rest of the ceremony. In other words, the greatest self-realization of my life was attained through loving relationships, through Pure Divine Love for my soul-family.

While connecting with each of them, a particular breathing technique was leading me. It was not always the same. Certain people helped me activate different chakras, and the breathing was different in such a way to make this happen. It was beyond my awareness.

As I connected with each of them, my heart was filled with infinite Love, tears of pure joy were falling down my face, and my smile was huge as I had never ever smiled before. As I was leaving a person, another breathing technique was taking over – same each time – and a void was created for a little while; and then, next...

The first one was my beloved spiritual teacher, Shaman Manin.
"I love you," I heard her voice.
"I love you too!"

Then, she gave me a mission, similar to the one in the *Lord of the Rings*. She gave me a sacred object and asked me to return it to the sacred temples of Tibet. I accepted, and saw myself accomplishing the mission. That told me (as in the *Lord of the Rings* movie) that my heart is pure and filled with love, so I won't buy into the temptation of keeping the sacred object for myself, and I'll also have the necessary protection, faith and determination to succeed.[1]

At the end of the mission, I looked at her (she was made of Light), we said "I love you!" to each other again, and left.

Total peace! Breathing and Void.

My grandmother Roza came to mind. She was right in front of me, and I told her, "Thank you so much for giving me the faith in Jesus!" I loved her spirit, and wanted to stay longer with her, but she transformed into a white dove, stayed in my hands for a few seconds, and then left. I love yooooooouuuuu..... Sadness took me over for a second, but then, I realized that she is in my heart forever, and the attachment of being connected with her in a certain way disappeared. I've learned a new level of *detached true love*. "When I am one with you, it doesn't matter that I don't have you. I am one with you forever!"

Bliss! Back to breathing and void. The seconds of total emptiness were longer and longer.

Next, Wanakhavi, my dear spiritual friend, came to mind. In my vision, he was a few feet away from me. I felt profound, deep, pure spiritual love. A green light burst out of my heart, and one came out of his, and our hearts merged and blended in a big, green Heart of Light, mid-distance, for a little while. That was the Magic Oneness Meditation I have channeled in the past. Thank you so much, Lord Shiva!

After a while, the green lights came back into our chests. This experience is something that we've experienced before during our group meditation, but not as pure and intense. For the first time, I saw a color – green. The pure spiritual love awakened to a deeper level in me. "This love is eternal, unconditional, and divine; it's the source of our mutual support for each other, through infinity!" Bliss! Tears of Joy!

Back to breathing and void.

My friend Geny came back in my vision. This time I connected to her in a different way. With my hands on her shoulders, I looked at her third eye and she looked at mine. I felt love, and almost completed the experience, but she said, "We didn't talk enough." Then I looked at her again, and my third eye started to spin spreading a rain of colors. Then, a light came out of my third eye, like a laser, spinning light toward her third eye, till our third eyes connected, then merged.

My heart was so full of love for her, I was in total bliss. By now I noticed that love felt for humans was the same as the love felt for my grandmother Roza, who had passed away. "Love is always pure, only people"s meanings make it feel different sometimes," I told myself. Our connection merged our experiences, and we both exploded in the shape of billions of colorful stars. "This is a new beginning." I thought.2

As soon as we exploded into blissful stars, I was back to breathing, then void.

Next, Jesus gave me a new heart. In my vision, His hand went through my physical body and inserted a big, shiny green, sparkling, full of life heart.
"Thank you, Jesus!"

Then, just for a second, I was the observer of my own future wedding – I saw myself beside a tall, slim man with short hair. Jesus married us.3

Next, I was with my father, giving him a head massage. My love for him was so blissful, tears of joy were pouring down my face. I gave him the gift of clairvoyance, by touching his third eye, and white and purple little stars were coming out of his third eye. He was relaxed, in total peace. He was happy. This was always my desire for him, and now he received the gift.4

Love! Bliss! Back to breathing and void.

Next, My Spirit Guides came into my awareness. I couldn't see them very well, but they gave me Spiritual Gifts. It felt like I had fireworks in my crown chakra. It was serene, but very short.

One of the women participating in the ceremony was wailing, reliving some bad memories that now were to be healed. The noise sent me from my guides directly into a hospital room, and there was my mom. She was in the worst shape I have ever seen her through the years. I looked at her, and said nothing, but gave her Light somehow, through all her body at once, and she was instantly healed. It was a miracle.

She was happy; she was *one* with her Higher Self. She was made of Light. She was the princess of the Christmas Party again – as she was at age fourteen, all pure, dressed in white, genuine. My love for her was transcending all barriers – she was healed! "O, my God! My mom is healed! This was the dream of my life, to help her heal, and now it was coming true, deep in my heart!"

Love! Fulfillment! Bliss! Back to breathing and void.

My friend Shahryar came to mind. We were in my copper pyramid in my apartment, meditating. I saw all his chakras, all colors. "That was a gift through Reiki" (he took all Reiki classes with me). Then I gave him a gemstone. As I put it in his hand, the stone started to pulse, then transformed into Light, then his hand transformed into white light, then all his body transformed into white light.

He was now my friend, *The White*. "Go home now, your family will be honored to see you, *The White*," I told him. Then, I visualized him in his home country, hugging his daughter, the light of his eyes.5

Harmony! Love! Bliss! Back to breathing and void.

My friend Adrian came to mind. His beautiful family was standing behind him. We held hands tight, like two friends who are making a pact. Our hands transformed into hands of light, we looked each other in the eyes, and knew that we'll be a support for each other through eternity. A deep connection and profound Soul-love burst in blissful colorful stars. Then, it disappeared.
Back to breathing and void.
Love! Fulfillment! Bliss!

My cousin Tania came to mind. She had short hair, as she had after her brain surgery. She was still not fully recovered, and I gave her a hug, and then, she was all filled with white light. She smiled, sharing love, then she disappeared.
Love! Bliss!

Back to breathing and void.

My friend Shakira came to mind. We were holding hands, and then we connected our hearts, and our sources of infinite joy. The Love was so pure; I gave her a white dove. The love was so deep, it sent me back to a past life where she was my younger sister and I saw her as a baby in my arms...
Love! Bliss!

Back to breathing and void.

An old man, with gray outfit, came to mind. I looked at him and recognized my cousin Tiberiu from Romania, who is currently young. It occurred to me that our meeting was taking place in a previous life. I looked at him, and touched my forehead to his, as we do when we meet, in a deep spiritual union. He instantly transformed in Light; it was him, *The White*. I told him: "You are one of the Spiritual Leaders of the World."
Love! Bliss!

Back to breathing and void.

Don Diego was singing different songs along the way, and playing different instruments. They were all in harmony with our experiences, at the very moment. It was a true blessing.

At some point, he was playing a song about Mother Earth.
I visualized myself hugging the planet Earth as if it were a pillow, and the planet was all surrounded in white light.

My teacher Alexandru came to my mind again. He didn't say "Focus, fetito" anymore. He said, "Thank you for allowing me to lead you on this journey. I was rewarded with more Light." Then I saw his huge globe of Light, as I'd seen it many times while praying for him in the past, but it was more powerful.

It was an ongoing connection, not a quick one, during the sacred ceremony, but now he was gone, out there in the Universe. No emotional bliss occurred, but the peace I felt was indescribable.

Don Diego prepared us for the closing of the Sacred Ceremony. I was searching, knowing that I wanted to see one more person at this time.
A bowl with green, fresh-grown grass came to my mind.

Then Elton, the man who saved my life and my soul when I was young, came to mind. He looked young, as he was when I met him. For some reason though, I felt like I had nothing with me to give him. But then, it occurred to me: "In spirit, I am *one* with God; I can create from nothing; I've been doing that with everyone, and created their gifts from nothing, I just didn't realize it."

So I looked at Elton, and told him, "Thank you so much for saving me. You saved a soul who now knows that it is *one* with God. Be blessed for eternity!" In the very next moment, Elton grew two huge white wings. He looked at me, smiled, and flew away.
I felt whole and complete.

"Do I want to go out there in the Universe?" I asked myself. The answer came, deep in my heart: "Who cares, it's all the same. Outward or inward, it's all *one*."

Don Diego was singing: "God is Love."

> *I am ONE with God. I create from nothing.*
> *I am Divine Love*
> ...
> *A new Beginning*

1: A few days later, sharing this experience with her, she said: "I didn't send you to the Tibetan temple, Councils did."

That night, the moment of her vision about Councils sending me to Tibet was matching the moment of my vision about her.

2: Next day I called her and told her about the experience. She was astonished to realize that she had been through a cleansing process all week, since I started to prepare for this ceremony, without knowing about it, that she connected with the symbols I was connected to; she was fasting the day before just like I did, and while having this experience, she first released negativity, and then she felt a new beginning. She had no explanation for all of this, but it shows clearly that the whole spiritual experience was real.

My gift for her was to take her with me fully on this journey, and it happened!
So, some might think that these experiences are illusions, but in fact the only illusion is to think that thoughts don't matter. They do, *"Thoughts are things."* And when they're combined with true love, they create powerfully, they create our reality.

3: Within the next three months I met my future husband and started to date him. For some reason though, the memory of my vision was blocked till our wedding day... That day, when I looked at our wedding photos, I remembered... my husband was the one in my vision... Jesus married us in spirit, before we even met.

4: A few days later I called my father who told me out of the blue that he started to feel his mom's presence... he is a very rational man, it was a big deal for him to say that... his psychic abilities started to blossom.

So I've asked myself this question: "What if all gifts I gave during the Sacred Ceremony are real? Creation through love... instant manifestation... I now have faith in instant healing, just like Jesus did. Not even touching, just a thought, and the receiver transforms in Light..."

5: He hadn't seen his beloved daughter right away, but soon he started to help people heal by giving them charged gemstones, filled with loving, healing light; he has been giving charged gemstones for children too, for the pure love in his heart is infinite, shining, and healing through the world.

The Tree of Life

"Did I really learn how to let go of my ego and have a pure spiritual experience?" I asked myself. Through the years, I have learned that in any new experience, the second time around I do it right. Below are my notes from my participation in the second Shamanic Ceremony:

The moment of dissolving the ego came; this time no resistance or confusion was there anymore, just the knowing that the ego is only the outfit for the eternal spirit; this time, "I" surrendered.

I love you, Sacred Plant; I welcome you; I am one with you.

Giving up the *"I" for "WE"* happened. "I" gave up any fear and limitations. The ego stepped aside.

In an instant, "I" felt how the Tree of Life embodied it. My hands transformed into branches and grew tall, piercing the ceiling. A purple-white-golden light went from the top of my head, up, through the ceiling, through the Universe, higher and higher… till a moment of fear almost stopped it.

The Universe…It's not too far, it's <u>one</u> – the voice of spirit said.

My spirit was one with the Tree of Life. The new me became *we*.
Roots were growing down from the feet, deep into the ground.

The tree must sit straight to hold the roots into the Earth.

We could see through the leaves' amazingly beautiful colors – purple, violet, blue, gold, green. A white light was coming down and up through the whole Universe...

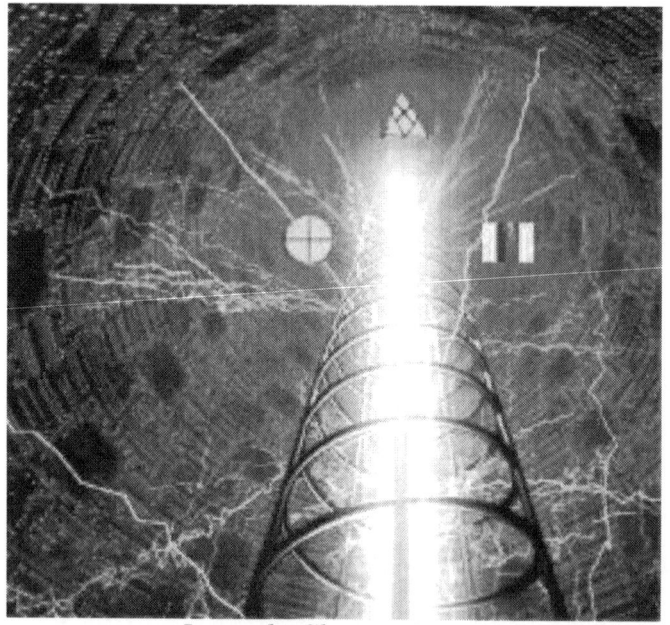

Image by Shaman Manin

Breathe. We are one. Breathe for us, the Sacred Plant commanded.

Saw lots of Sacred Eastern symbols; beautiful colors... violet, blue, and white, golden, green...

Let me be us

Learn how to love, or you'll play out of tune! Imagine how an out-of-tune sound would be heard through the whole Universe. When one plays in harmony, out of love, the whole Tree vibrates in a beautiful song; all the others need to do is to listen, and they will be mesmerized...

We pulled in a galaxy and enjoyed the brilliant colors. The galaxy is now just a cell of our body...

Now I understand how Don Diego can help us: we are all inside the same tree of life.
All of us in the circle are sitting against the bark of the tree of life, on the inside.

My beloved and I met in spirit and meditated at the candle, just the way we do every day in the physical world. The light was different than the regular candle's light: a big globe of Light, with lots of violet and white in it. We were *one* in spirit. We went out into the Universe through the ceiling together.

*

We are one and must be all healed

It was time for *us* to do some healing.
We are doing healing on my beloved's solar plexus. He had a hole in it from another lifetime and that's how he died. Now *we* see golden light inside.
He needs love. That's all the medicine he needs. The Sacred Plant said.

My mom came. She pulled out of her chest an old pain. Fill the empty space with Light!

Release everything, be free!
My mom is being cleansed, flipped from one side to the other by leaves.

My father came. *Our* leaves are surrounding his head; his temples were gently touched and his tiredness taken away. My father was happy.
Then, my parents were cleansed by *the leaves* together.

As my parents were healed, a Light went straight to my uterus; O my God, my uterus is filled with light! I love you, mother and father!
We are all hugging with much love.

We called Harry and Miriam together and made them one big tree. Their girls came at the bottom of the trunk. The younger one kind of melted in, but the older one came to me and hugged me. "Thank you, Angel! Thank you, God-daughter! *We* love you! *We* put a crown of Light on your head. Go embrace your family, now is peace."

Geny needs healing. She came in front of the Tree. *We* pulled her inside the Tree and gave her healing. She will be with *us* for the remainder of the ceremony. She energetically threw up all her blockages.

Our God-daughter came back and asked *us* to help her parents more. Okay baby, watch this: they are being cleansed deeply. Harry is screaming out old anger till he finds relief.

We are *one* with Miriam. I feel her pain. She screamed and screamed… and let go of all her old pain. Miriam, put a hand on your heart and say:

I love myself
I forgive myself
I am at peace with myself
And
I love you
I forgive you
I am at peace with you

"Miriam, give thanks to Shaman Manin and Councils." Healing continued... "Miriam, forgive yourself... you have given birth to children of Light. Connect deeply with our Mother Earth."

Now she's going back to Harry and sees him in a different light. They are kissing with much love.

Dan came to *us*.
Release through your roots! Pull out your pain. It comes from childhood. Look up and see your light piercing through the ceiling and your branches growing through the Universe...You are really getting it! Be blessed.

Jade came to *us*. *Our* leaves surrounded her head. She pulled her pain out of her head. "Relax! You are free and you have wings, angel; *We* love you."

Our God-daughter came back again!
She wants healing for herself!
I am releasing for her, with her, with my mouth opened, breathing out convulsively.
Our leaves healed her; she came out made of Light.
Thank you, Sacred Plant! Thank you, God! "I love you so much, it is an honor to take on your suffering and release it for you. You are teaching me true love. Thank you!"

Dalia came to *us*.
She sat in front of the Tree. I released for her; pain came out of her – pain from miscarriage, pain from divorce; I can relate to both traumas. The leaves of The Tree of Life cleansed her deeply, till light was shining in her house. Then The Tree of Life, made of Light, grew through her house.

Thank you, Don Diego! It is hard to release for all, but *we* can!

We are releasing for all of us in the room and looking up to the colorful lights, through galaxies. Then *we* put our roots deep into the ground.

We are all given a huge blessing of bright light. All of us in the room are *lights*. The energy starts to spiral between us, and inside the Tree of Life, is going upwards like the Kundalini serpent, for all at once.

The Ocean needs healing. Mother Earth, please calm *our* waves from the bottom up.

Our Mother Earth is pregnant. She will give birth to itself. She needs healing.
The leaves surrounded our Mother Earth and healed her till the Light was on inside.
Now it is peace.

We release for all our branches, for all our past lives. Our leaves are falling and rebirthing. New branches and leaves of Light are now growing.

*

Nothing is for us, everything is through us

We are giving our teachers Bob and Manin a blessing of profound thanks.

We give thanks to *our* teacher's soul. Alexandru is in a Sacred Temple of Light – white, violet, golden – in Heaven. He sits in meditation posture, and he's very focused and sharp, and powerful, and peaceful… Thank you Alexandru!

My sweetheart's and my roots of Light meet under the ground again… there is Light and all colors dancing in our union. Our whole being is dancing on Don Diego's music.

The west and ancient east are one – the voice of Spirit said.

Next, our beloved Shaman from the east invokes Lord Shiva, from the west, in his song. He unites the Apus and Tibetan energies through his pure spirit, and we are all grasping that oneness through his songs.
We feel total relief.
We see the hand of Shiva with the thumb and middle finger touching, and Light coming out of his hand. We are a big pyramid. Lord Shiva is inside the pyramid…inside *our* soul.

After a while, the Shaman closes the ceremony. Thank you, Don Diego!

*

Even my ego enjoyed: "It was the most beautiful experience of my life! Now I know who I am: a servant for this soul; I love you."

God, *thank you* for making us and giving us light! We are blissful! We are grateful. We are *one*!

The "I" is back, but is not the same. It is grateful, peaceful, and content.
"Thank you God for working miracles through me for all these wonderful people."

My roots are roots of Light. Thank you all for healing yourselves. We are *one*. Let's focus on our roots and fruits of light; they are growing through the Universe.

My pen stopped writing. Even though insights were pouring out, after a few minutes, I stopped trying.

I watched the stars shining through the branches of the trees for a while, and then I went to sleep. The Sacred Ceremony started again for a while, in my dreams. I don't remember, but I know that my soul does.

Thank you Sacred Plant.
Thank you Don Diego.
Thank you God!

Trinity

For a long time, I wanted to understand the significance of Trinity. I wanted that profoundly important understanding. Something was telling me that I will better tune into the spiritual energies and better serve everyone in need.

This is what I decided to make my only teaching request of my last Sacred Plant Ceremony. Don Diego is a perfect teacher through his own profound understanding of Trinity, both in Christianity (The Father, The Son, and The Holy Spirit) and in Hinduism (Brahma, Vishnu, Shiva).

This time I planned to give up writing down any inspiring messages from spirit during the ceremony, any extraordinary outward universal experiences, and look only for the deepest meaning and for being of service for the highest good.

Don Diego planned for this ceremony to lead us into planetary healing. The 2012 shift in consciousness was approaching and it was essential to focus on the highest good of humankind, and on the highest good of our planet.

We sat quietly in our sacred spaces and one by one, went to the Shaman to bless us and to give us Sacred Plant to drink. After a while, Mother Vine awakened in me.

> *Ayahuasca in the pot is the same as Jesus saying "Drink my blood"* I heard.

What does that mean?
Mother Vine is being cut, smashed, boiled for a week under intense prayers and sacred ceremony, and then ingested, assimilated in our bodies. By drinking it, we become one with it, and only then can she pull out our pains, heal our wounds from the past, purify us, show us our essence, and help us grow in spirit.

Jesus said "Drink my blood," and the metaphor is to allow His essence, His spirit into ourselves, to let Him work through us and heal us, and teach us, and raise us to the highest peaks of spiritual evolution.

In the same way, HH the Dalai Lama was teaching us to meditate and imagine that we are ingesting the Divine "nectar" coming down from our Masters, and we let the Divine Bliss dissolve us and manifest into us.
It's the Universal Law of Union with the Divine, of renunciation of identifying ourselves with our egos.

For a little while, Mother Vine made her presence known in me again in the shape of the Tree of Life. The Tree of Life made fruits of Light; they fell on the land and from each one a Being of Light emerged. We are fruits of Light of the Tree of Life. And children are the true abundance of Life.

It doesn't matter if you cut a branch or a root, the same imbalance occurs for the tree. Branches are roots into the Father Sky.
Roots are roots into the Mother Earth.
In between, I am.

My roots of light grew wide, and far away from them grew new trees. What a beautiful, fertile and spiritually rich image. Thank you, Sacred Plant.

Opening my eyes, I looked straight ahead at my image of Jesus, and focused on it.
Jesus from the image in front of me grew seven meters tall, and came closer and blessed me.
I am at peace, profound peace.

I asked to learn about Trinity.

The answer came with the clarity of deep waters.
1. With fingers together on your forehead, look up, breathe in deeply and say "In the name of the Father"; this way you bring all the blessings and energies from God.
2. With fingers together on your heart, look down, breathe out and say "In the name of the Son"; this way you release for that person to be healed, just like Jesus did on the cross; you send them healing from the center of the Sacred Heart.
3. With fingers together on the right shoulder, come back to a posture of straight back. Breathe in and say "In the name of the Holy Spirit." The Holy Spirit brings you comfort and restores your balance. You must understand, you need good care for yourself and everyone you serve.
4. With fingers together on your left shoulder, breathe out and say "Amen." Seal the energies.

When the Father works, the Son rests.
When the Son works, the Father rests.
The Father Creates. The Son manifests.

I was sent directly into practical training and exercised Trinity for the next few hours.
Many people came for healing. Some of them were in my thoughts before the Sacred Ceremony; others had not been in my thoughts for many years. It was challenging to see all their issues, known and unknown in real life.

In the beginning I had the tendency to get involved emotionally in their trauma, to process it and release it, but I was told by Mother Vine that emotional involvement is unnecessary. *Just do the symbol of the Holy Cross and follow the Trinity recipe.*
And so I did for many people, one by one.

I stood up like a tree for a long time. At times, people's pain felt like cuts and shakes in the tree of life. Leaves were shaking.

To maintain balance of body, mind, and spirit, I kept my left hand with palm up and my right hand in a prayer posture in front of my heart. That helped me center myself.

At times I was drawing the Reiki Symbols for the person who was receiving healing. Not even they were necessary – I was told. *They are included in the power of Trinity. This recipe works for the whole Universe.*

At times I forgot to comfort myself. I was getting lost in the first and second steps, with the full dedication of a giver, till I was almost in danger, forgetting to breathe. Every time I was reminded by spirit: *remember yourself*; and then I would stay with the Holy Spirit for a while or I would do Trinity for my own rejuvenation.

One of the participants across from where I was sitting was brought to me in spirit. *Heal this man from drinking me, and tell him that I will be with him forever* – Mother Vine said. At the end of the ceremony, I asked him how many times he participated. He said, "thirty times."

That didn't sound right to me; I had never met someone who participated thirty times before. Mother Vine surely gave me the right message. I shared my vision, placed a hand on his heart and sent him another ray of light.

The healing expanded from people to places, trees, forests, authorities, ancestors, grandmothers and great-grandmothers from different lands, from different continents.

The ocean needed healing, and in the name of the Father, and in the name of the Son, received sparks of light and transformed into a shiny, turquoise, peaceful infinity of waters.

Our dear Shaman needed comforting and rejuvenation – he had been so dedicated to people's spiritual evolution for so many years, he put aside his own life.

Mother Vine needed healing too… She has seen so much suffering; she has sacrificed herself to go deep inside our roots and process out all our pains. For a second, I gave into that empathic suffering, and only the voice of spirit was able to bring me back. It was really intense.

Mother Earth received healing. The whole planet is like a cherry in a child's hand.
In the name of the Father…
In the name of the Son…

In the name of the Holy Spirit...
Amen!

The devil showed up wanting to take one of my dearest people in my life. In an instant, Shaman Manin's teachings came to mind – I offered him Love – Forgiveness – Peace. I offered healing, and more Love – Forgiveness – Peace, till he left without taking anyone.

After that I needed more comforting for myself... I wanted to rest but Don Diego kept singing powerful healing songs, leading me into action.

The stars... our friends from other planets... they appeared through clouds and gray dust, up in the sky, in need of healing.
The Trinity recipe worked for them too! The Son does not love only us, here on Earth. The *Son loves everyone.*

Three times, "fuel" needed to be burned. Since I didn't travel outside of my body, Kundalini had to come out another way. I was breathing out flames from time to time, between healing sessions.
Shaman Manin was there in spirit telling me: "Give me the fuel, I'll use it." And she was breathing it in, and then she was blowing out stars of Light, doing healing in other dimensions, other galaxies, sending Love – Forgiveness – Peace.

Days after the ceremony, we were talking on the phone and she told me that while I was in the ceremony, she slept the whole time and went so far out into the Universe, she doesn't remember where she was...she just knew that she was in service, for the highest good.

I am so grateful for this sacred teamwork. My teacher, you are so sublime!

Jesus processing and releasing humans' suffering on the cross flooded my entire being… It was one of the most profound and intense experiences of my life.
"Father, please heal your Son. I love you so much, Jesus!"

Don Diego started a Puja Sacred Ceremony, inside the Sacred Plant Ceremony.
We were all worshiping Lord Shiva. The "dust" of our lives and of everyone who came in spirit for healing was swept away. Destruction of the old and re-creation in Light took place, indeed, for all of us. Thank you, Lord Shiva! Amazingly powerful and beautiful energies were uplifting our hearts, our spirits, and our world. Bliss and Unity! Transformation!

> Thank You God
> Thank you Don Diego
> Thank you Sacred Plant
> Amen!

*

That was a truly Focused on Spirit experience… now it was time to come back to a Focused on Spirit day-by-day life.

Jesus left so His loving followers can find Him inwardly. My first teacher, Alexandru, left, and yes, as a loving student, I can connect with him inwardly.

If I never have the opportunity to be in a Sacred Plant Ceremony with Shaman Diego again, I will always find him and Mother Vine inwardly.

Who is "I" and what is "inward"?
Usually the "I" is the ego – a very obedient one, who has learned to focus on spirit.

As long as we are on Earth, the best friend or the best enemy of our spirit is our ego.

Let's make sure our ego is our soul's best friend, and let's live a life Focused on Spirit.

Amen!

About the Author

Laura O'Neale is a Reiki Master/Teacher, Shaman in training, Certified Massage Therapist and Meditation Techniques Guide. Her soul mission is to heal and teach through spiritual love. She knows that we are all beloved children of the Universe, and she has been called to assist the seekers toward their happiness.

Laura earned a Bachelor's Degree in Computer Science in Romania, her home country. Currently, she resides in Washington, D.C. However, she considers herself a universal soul, because people around the world have a home in her heart.

Please visit Laura at www.YourLightWithin.com

For events, classes or other services provided by Laura, or to purchase Laura's books online, please visit www.YourLightWithin.com

Laura's books:

The Journey of the Colorful Stars
A Pathway toward Love, Faith and Healing

&

Reiki and the Path to Enlightenment
A Reiki and Shamanic Journal for Energy Healing Students, Practitioners and Teachers

&

Focused on Spirit
A Journal about Spiritual Gifts Serving Humanity